Magic Wool Mermaids, Fairies and Nymphs Through the Seasons

Magic Wool Mermaids, Fairies and Nymphs Through the Seasons

Christine Schäfer

Floris Books

Translated by Anna Cardwell

Photographs by Stefan Schäfer
Drawings by Christine Schäfer

First published in German under the title
Feen, Nymphen, Nixen by Verlag Freies Geistesleben in 2011
This English edition was first published in 2014
Second printing 2016

© 2011 Verlag Freies Geistesleben, Stuttgart
This translation © Floris Books 2014

British Library CIP Data available
ISBN 978-178250-038-4
Printed in Malaysia

Contents

About Fairies and the Seasons

To understand the book of nature,
you must wander through its pages
on your own two feet.

Paracelsus

Nature is like a colourful picture book, opening a new page month after month. If you look carefully, every season offers something special to see. Whether you live in the countryside or the city, each season has its own gifts and beauty to treasure.

The changing seasons have left their mark on our culture, and myths and festivals celebrating them have become part of many people's lives. Often these festivals have a long-standing tradition and an even older pagan origin.

Beautiful stories have also evolved around nature and its four seasons. Many myths and legends of nature spirits, goddesses, witches and fairies have survived to the present day in fairy tales and fables; for example, the Brothers Grimm fairy tales are based on old folk stories. Thinking of these ancient tales and the turning of the seasons can bring lots of inspiration for creative work.

The idea of a seasonal table was developed in Waldorf teaching to celebrate the joy of nature, even indoors. It doesn't have to be a large display; a small table, a shelf, or a large plate can be decorated to capture the important aspects of the different seasons. You can arrange a beautiful scene to suit the time of year, or make an entire miniature world with your children – it is up to you.

Either way, it's fun selecting a theme for making a new figure, and deciding how you want to depict it. Just choose your favourite from the selection of fairies and mythical characters in the following pages.

I hope this book gives you lots of inspiration.

With all good wishes
Christine Schäfer

About this Book

"How do you make figures that stand up?" I have been asked this question more than any other in recent years, and this book gives the answer. The first chapters give information about materials and techniques. Later chapters show detailed instructions for making individual figures.

First, I would like to share some general ideas about needle felting for any beginners among you. In recent years felting has found more and more enthusiastic fans. Felting courses are offered everywhere, and there is a great assortment of beautiful materials now available. Wool, the material used for felting, is experiencing a boom unimaginable just a decade ago.

Besides the ancient technique of wet felting, which is used for high-quality everyday items and wearable textiles, needle felting is also becoming widespread. Using special needles, wool is compacted and compressed. This method is easy to learn. In contrast to wet felting (which requires hot water, soap and a waterproof felting surface), needle felting can be done almost anywhere. The materials required are easy to transport and the workspace remains clean apart from a few fluffs of wool. There are no waste products.

The figures shown in this book are primarily made for decoration. Whether for a seasonal tableau, a Christmas window, a corner of a child's room or a wedding table, you can make wonderful figures for any event or festival.

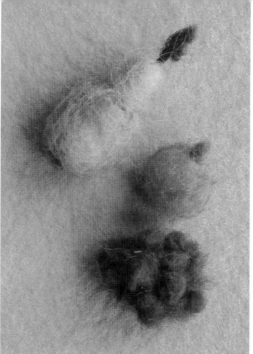

Please note, the figures in this book are not toys; they contain small parts and young children can pull some of the figures apart even when carefully wound around an inner wire frame. If you want to make figures for children to play with, use a more sturdy wire frame and wet felt the figures with water and soap. Remember that wool shrinks, and you will need some experience to achieve a well-proportioned figure. Older children are more careful and can use needle felted and wound figures for making a seasonal table or decorating a favourite corner in their room.

The technique I use here is a combination of winding and needle felting. Step-by-step instructions show the techniques for making different figures, requiring varying degrees of skill. In this book I have explained the figures in detail so that beginners can quickly achieve good results.

The topics of wool production, preparation and dyeing have been dealt with in numerous other publications. In this book I will simply describe the different types of wool suitable for making the figures described in this book. I have included a chapter containing simple techniques for dyeing small amounts of wool.

Each step-by-step instruction includes a list of all materials needed for the figure. The degrees of difficulty are indicated with ✳✳✳.

Skill rating

Easy ✳
Medium ✳✳
Experienced ✳✳✳

Fleece	Roving

Rough	Fine

Tools and Techniques

Magic wool

'Magic wool' is a term used to describe dyed unspun sheep's wool. Magic wool is plant dyed, relatively airy wool fleece of a coarse quality. The figures depicted in this book have been made using wool from different breeds of sheep. If you enjoy experimenting, you can also try using camel, mohair or alpaca wool.

For dry felting you can use almost any quality and type of wool. Wool can be purchased in varying quality, either processed into large bats or carded into long strands and sold as roving. Bats and roving contain long and short fibres and sometimes pieces of leftover organic material. Nowadays you can also obtain beautiful multi-coloured wool combined with silk strands, which give the material a beautiful shine.

Ready-packaged wool can be found in many craft shops or Steiner-Waldorf school markets. Many internet sites offer a large range of loose wool, usually sold by weight. (See Resources at the end of the book.) For some of the figures I use a coarser wool quality, e.g. Scottish wool or New Zealand wool, generally plant dyed in harmonious, soft colours. Other figures are made out of synthetically dyed merino wool, which is sold in many strong colour ranges.

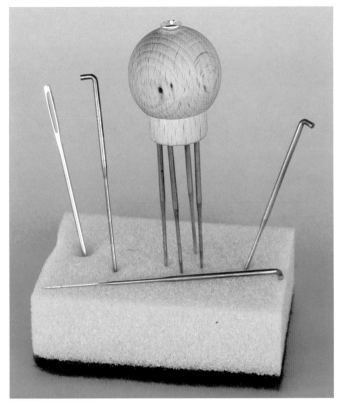

The figures in this book are between 10 cm (4 in) and 20 cm (8 in) high, so you will only need small amounts of each colour. For this reason, ready-sorted coloured packaged wool is good. Never discard leftover wool – it can always be used for details!

As well as carded fleece there are also uncarded nubs – these are sheep's curls which come in different shapes and sizes, depending on the breed of sheep. Wensleydale, Leicester and Gotland give particularly beautiful, shiny curls. Many of the hairstyles for the small figures in this book are made with these curls. Usually you can buy the curls ready dyed.

You can also dye the nubs yourself. I have shown several simple dyeing methods which can be done in your kitchen with very little effort. Since the nubs are not carded, they often contain bits of hay and straw, which need to be removed carefully by hand. The bee children (page 74) are an example of making hair with nubs.

A final tip for working with wool: never cut wool with scissors! Tease it and pull it apart gently. The more slowly you pull, the more easily the wool will separate.

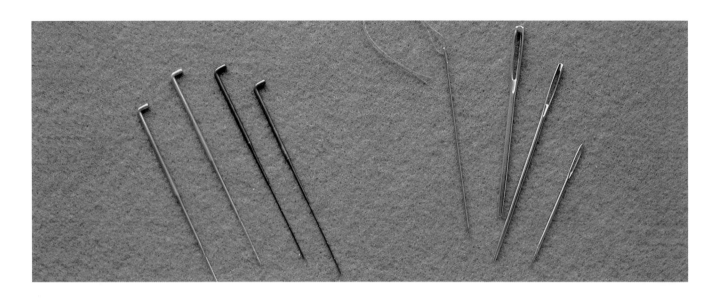

Felting needles

Felting needles are special needles with small barbed hooks at the tip, which felt single wool fibres together. Always have several needles to hand as they can break easily during use. They come in different sizes, but I prefer using medium sized needles for the figures described in this book. Felting needles are very useful and convenient for attaching hair, correcting a figure's shape and attaching decorative parts and wings. They are also useful for re-attaching stray strands of wool in place.

Hold the needle at the top and always poke down vertically. The needle will break easily if bent. To get a better grip on the needle, you can use a needle holder, which holds one or several needles simultaneously. They allow large surfaces of wool to be felted quickly, but are rarely needed for making figures. Take care when using a felting needle tool, as it is much easier to prick your finger than with a single felting needle.

For the felting surface, use a sponge at least 4 cm (1½ in) thick. You can easily start off with a dense household sponge, moving to a Styrofoam board for larger projects. Alternatively, special felting brushes are sold in specialist shops or on the internet. Needle felting foam mats, sold in craft stores, make a more pleasant felting surface and they are also more durable. Work out which felting surface works best for you.

You will need a felting surface and felting needle for each figure described in this book. As you should always keep these tools handy, I have not included them in the lists of materials. You will also need a sewing needle, skin-coloured sewing thread, white craft glue, rhinestone glue or fabric glue and a pair of scissors for cutting out decorative parts.

Nubs of wool

Washed   Dirty

Dyeing

It can be difficult finding wool nubs for a particular fairy in the exact shade you want, so it helps to know how to dye your own curly wool. I felt it was too much effort colouring a handful of nubs using professional methods, so I tried to find a simple solution. I use the techniques described below for dyeing small amounts of wool nubs and have achieved wonderful results. The materials needed for dyeing are found in household stores or supermarkets. Choose the dyeing method which best suits your requirements.

Dyed nubs

Onion skins, beetroot juice, dried blueberries, tea and coffee were the first ideas I tried out. Onion skins gave beautiful effects, with a range of colours from reddish brown to light yellow resulting from a single dye bath. Here are the instructions for dyeing with onion skins.

RECIPE

- Skins from 5–6 large onions (use only the dry outer skins)
- 500 ml (17 fl oz) water

Boil the ingredients in a small pot and leave it to simmer with the lid on for an hour. Pour the mixture through a fine sieve to remove all the skin. Pour the mixture back into the pot and add a handful of pre-washed nubs (I use a mild shampoo to wash the nubs). Boil again and leave the nubs in the dye bath for up to an hour. The longer and hotter the process is, the more intense the colour becomes. Make sure the nubs are completely immersed in the dye. Do not stir or the nubs will felt!

When you are happy with the colour, remove the nubs from the dye bath and wash them out briefly in cold water. Use a towel to absorb excess water from the nubs, and place them in a warm place to dry. You can re-use the dye bath to make lighter shades of the same colour. This makes beautifully natural hair colours.

You can also experiment with other plant dyes. Birch leaves give shades of yellow, dried walnut leaves produce a beautiful blond-brown colour. Experiment as much as you please; it is always fun and the results can be surprising!

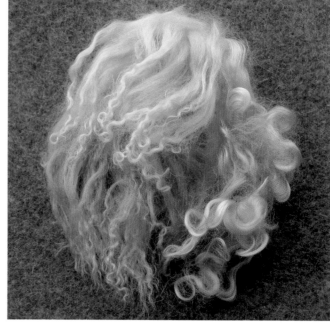

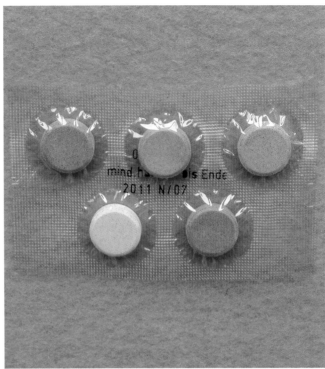

Dyeing with food colours

Food dyes are another simple way to colour wool nubs. This basic recipe will get you started.

RECIPE

- Colour tablets or food dye in your chosen colour
- Approximately 300 ml (10 fl oz) of water
- One serving spoon of vinegar

Boil the ingredients in a small cooking pot and add a handful of washed nubs. Boil again and leave the wool in the dye bath for up to half an hour. The longer you leave the wool in, and the hotter the dye bath is, the more intense the colour will be. Immerse the wool completely for an even colour or leave the wool floating for interesting colour effects. Do not stir or the nubs will felt!

Once the curls have dyed sufficiently, remove them from the dye bath and rinse with cold water until the water runs clear. Absorb excess water with a towel and dry in a warm place. Mix the leftover dye baths for interesting colour shades. Use the colour circle by Johannes Itten on page 42 to help you find matching colours. A weak dye bath gives a pastel shade.

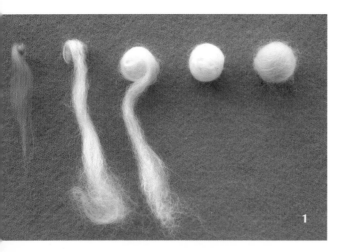

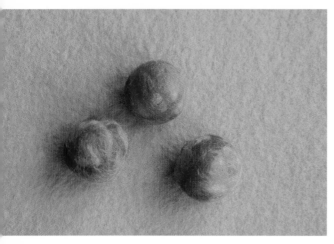

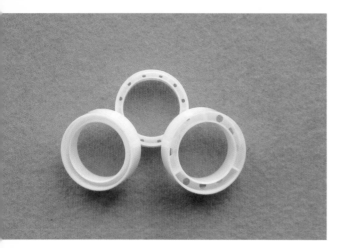

For beginners

This section is written for beginners. If you are already an expert at felting and have experience making wool figures, skip the following pages and start making a figure!

Before making a figure, it is necessary to practise handling and using magic wool. Beginners often work the wool for a long time with their hands, and for some wool types (e.g. fine merino), this can lead to unwanted felting. Once you have mastered the basic techniques described below it will be easy to follow the instructions for the standing fairies. It is worthwhile investing some time to practise the necessary skills, and the ideas described below will make practising more varied and interesting.

Exercise 1: Making a small wool ball

Wind a small amount of wool into a tight ball, then wind more layers around it. This is the same principle as winding a ball of yarn. Poke the felting needle into the ball repeatedly to stop the layers slipping. Repeat this process until you have achieved the desired circumference and firmness (figure 1).

A tip from my felting courses

Even with a correctly sized pattern, it is difficult to make an exact sized ball for the head. To avoid this problem, I give my students an empty sticky tape roll with an inner circumference the correct size for the inner ball of a fairy head – that is, 2½ cm (1 in). The firm wool ball should easily fit through the hole.

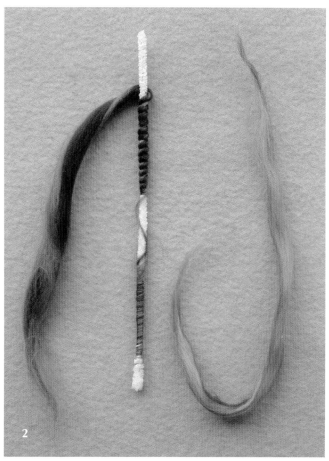

Exercise 2: Tying off a strand of wool

Take a very thin length of wool fibre and wind it firmly around the centre of a wool strand to bind it off (figure 1). Keep your fingers on the wool fibre close to the winding point; this allows you to pull tight without breaking the fibres. Wind the wool right to the last fibre. In the beginning, you can use sewing thread for binding off if the wool fibres keep breaking.

Exercise 3: Winding wool around wire

Carefully wind a strand of wool around a pipe cleaner (figure 2). Make sure you do not twist the wool while winding, as you will make unattractive rolls that tend to slip off the wire. The single strands of wool should not be too thick – this helps you get a nice even smooth winding. Twist the pipe cleaner slowly between your fingers, and you will find the correct winding technique is quite simple.

17

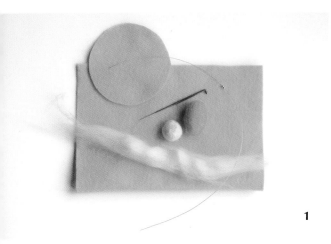

1

2

3

BEADS

With some practice, you can make beautiful wool balls in all colours and sizes. To felt them into beautiful and durable beads, put them in a washing net bag and wash in the washing machine at 60 °C (140 °F).

You can even make cute little gnomes with two felt balls and a small pointy hat (figures 1–3). Cut a quarter circle out of felt, and glue or sew up the sides. Sew the hat to the smaller ball, thread the balls together with strong embroidery thread and knot the ends. To make more durable gnomes, use jewellery wire instead of embroidery thread. You can then decorate the hat and body.

Things to make with tied-off strands of wool

MINIATURE BUNNIES

Fold the tied-off strand of wool in half and tie it off again twice, as shown in figure 4. This makes a small, stylised rabbit. Felt the head to the back with a few pokes of the felting needle and rub the tips of the ears between your fingers to shape them. I made the small rabbit on page 62 in this way.

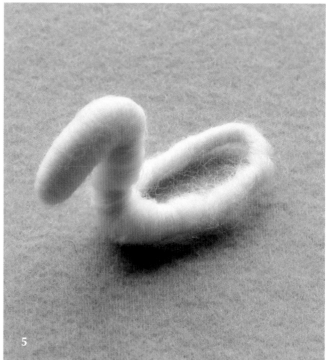

Things to make out of pipe cleaners covered with wool

SHEEP LYING DOWN

To make a sheep lying down, bend wire covered in white, brown or beige wool into the shape shown in figure 5. Wind more and more wool around the body to make a fluffy sheep (figure 6). Wool bat and nubs are good for this. To finish, felt a small tuft of wool around the head and add ears.

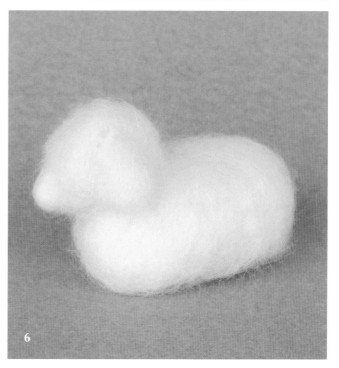

Making a Body and Clothes

Once you have mastered the basic exercises in the previous chapter, you are ready to start making different figures. There are several ways of making standing figures.

Simple Figures are made without a solid wool base and have a wood stand instead. They can be placed in clay flowerpots to help them stand up.

Standing Figures have a solid, stable framework so that they can stand on their own. They require some skill and you will need more wool to make them.

Simple figures *

It is quite simple to felt small figures in flowerpots. Once you have mastered the basic principles, you can make new variations of small shoots and flower children.

Shoots *

MATERIALS

- Skin-coloured and natural brown wool
- Light green craft felt for the leaves
- Sewing needle and light green sewing thread
- A small clay pot, diameter 5 cm (2 in)

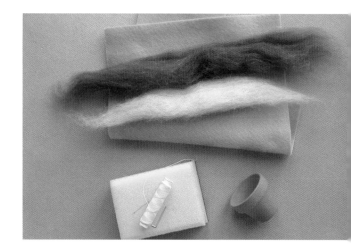

Shoots are just little figures with a head. They are very easy to make.

Start by making the head. Make a skin-coloured ball, approximately 2 cm (1 in) diameter (see Exercise 1, p.16). Make sure the ball is not too soft. If you press the ball between your fingertips, it should only give a little. Place the ball on to a tied-off, skin-coloured strand of wool (see Exercise 2). The strand of wool should be between 15 cm (6 in) and 20 cm (8 in) long and not too thick. About a quarter of the wool roving should be enough. Wind the strand of wool tightly around the ball and wind some wool fibres firmly around the neck several times. The tied-off spot should be at the very top of the head. Make sure the wool fibres covering the face are spread out smoothly and evenly.

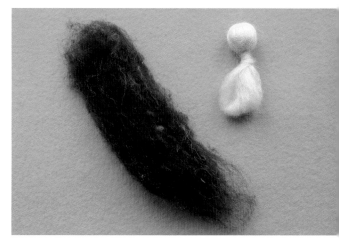

Cut the shoots out of a piece of light green craft felt. Cut a strip of felt 1 cm (½ in) by 6½ cm (2–3 in) long. Round off the corners. Sew this double leaf to the top of the head.

Wind brown wool around the ends of the skin-coloured wool below the neck for 'potting earth' (figure 2 overleaf). Needle felt in place by poking

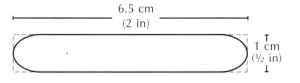

6.5 cm
(2 in)

1 cm
(½ in)

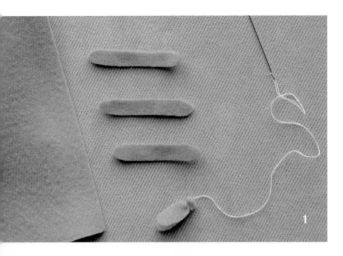

into the wool repeatedly. Make sure the neck remains free. Wind several layers of brown wool and needle felt the brown wool into a conical shape to fit into the flowerpot.

To finish, wind the wool for the hair around the head and then needle felt into place (figure 3). Take care not to poke all the way through the head to the face! Pull the shoots into shape.

Now all you need to do is plant the shoot into the flowerpot!

Simple standing figures **

This is a simple method for making figures that stand up. You can make the wooden stands in different sizes, and place the figures on as desired. When the figures are removed from the stands, they can be stored until needed again. These stands are also ideal for displaying a favourite fairy or guardian angel for a short time – for example on a Christmas display or for a birthday.

Wooden stands

MATERIALS
- Wood or bamboo skewers
- Circles of wood or wooden wheels in different sizes
- Pliers, cutter or small saw
- Wood glue or craft glue
- If necessary, hand drill or drill

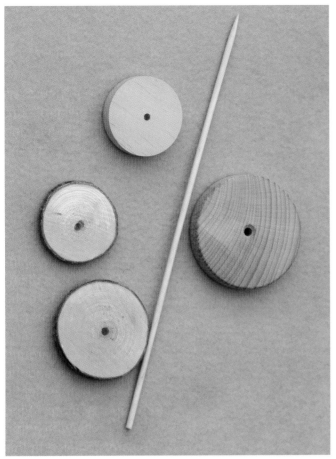 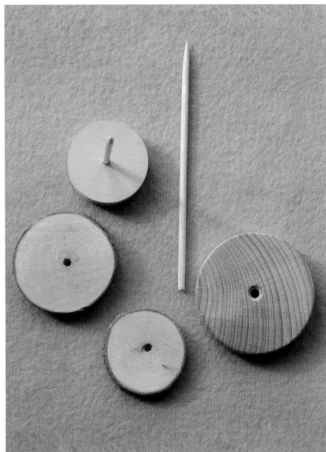

You can find skewers in any supermarket. Wood or craft glue and small wooden wheels in a variety of sizes can be purchased in craft shops and DIY shops. Wheels already have a hole drilled in the centre and making the stand with them is very easy. Florists sell simple wood slices, sometimes with the bark still attached. The wood is dry and they are inexpensive, but you will need to drill a hole through the centre. You can also saw your own wood segments, if you have the tools and skills!

Shorten the skewer to the desired length with the cutter or pliers and glue it vertically to the hole in the wood slice. Allow the glue to dry fully before placing a figure on the stand.

For small figures, make your stand about 2–3 cm (1 in) diameter; stick length about 5–6 cm (2 in).

Large figures need a stand about 4–5 cm (1–2 in) diameter, stick length about 10–12 cm (4–5 in).

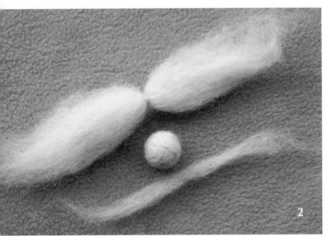

Making the inner body

The basic structure of all the wool figures is the same, regardless of size. First, make a skin-coloured inner core, then add the clothes and decorative parts.

MATERIALS
- Skin-coloured wool
- One pipe cleaner, about 15 cm (6 in)

Start by making the **head**. You will need a skin-coloured head, approximately 2½ cm (1 in) diameter for a large fairy (Exercise 1, p.16). Make the head in the same way as for the simple figures (see instructions on page 20).

To attach the **arms**, lay the pipe cleaner around the finished head. Bend the wire once around the strand of wool below the neck and pull as tightly as possible so that it cannot slip any more. Wind around the torso crosswise repeatedly with a thin strand of wool (figure 7). The arms created in this way should be of equal length (figure 6).

Now you can wind wool around the hands and arms. Take a very thin strand of skin-coloured wool and start winding at one end of the pipe cleaner. Bend the wire back after approximately 1 cm (½ in) to make the hand. Take a further strand and wind completely up the arm, evenly and smoothly (see Exercise 3, p.17). Make sure you cannot see the pipe cleaner through the wool, particularly at the hands. If necessary, wind around any exposed parts once more with a small tuft of wool. Repeat for the other arm (figures 8 and 9).

25

 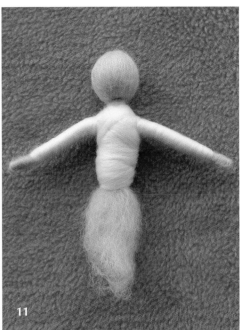 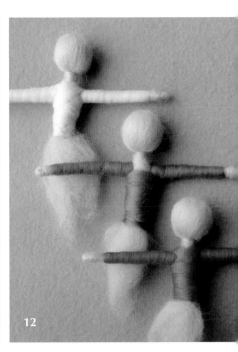

Wind crosswise around the body again. Wind firmly and right to the last piece of the wool. You can vary the head size and arm length, depending on the desired size of the finished figure.

Now decide what kind of lower body you want for your figure.

Making the clothes

Firstly, dress the figures with a top. Naturally you can have different lengths and shapes of tops. If you want to make short sleeves, wind an additional layer of skin-coloured wool around the arms to make a natural looking arm shape.

MATERIALS
• Wool in the colour of your choice

Starting at the wrist, wind a thin layer of coloured wool around the arm. Leave out the hands (figure 10). Wind three to four thin layers of wool around the entire arm. Make the layers thicker towards the top to give the arm a realistic shape. Repeat on the other side. Carefully wind around the body crosswise. Make sure the strand of wool does not twist and is wound evenly and firmly around the body (figures 11 and 12).

Shape the entire figure with the felting needle and make small corrections if necessary.

To make the **dress**, use about 30 cm (12 in) of coloured wool roving. Different types of wool can vary in thickness. If the roving is too sparse, you may have to take a double layer so that the

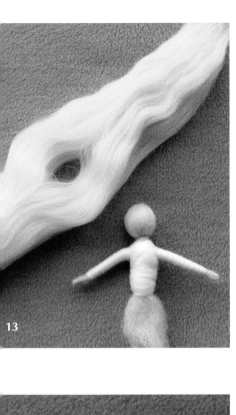

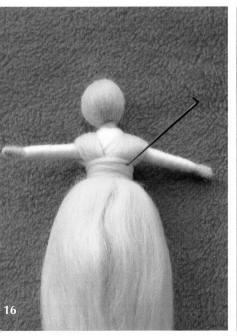

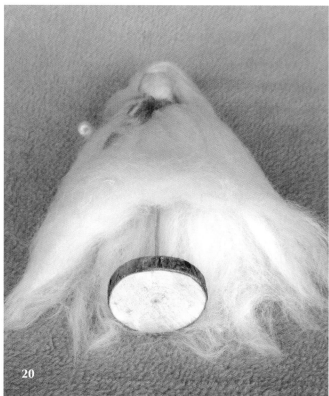

figure does not look too thin. Thick roving can be reduced in volume a little. To do this, pull away a section of the wool over the entire length. Make an opening in the centre of the wool strand (figure 13). Push the head through this opening (figure 14). Arrange the strand of wool over the shoulders and over the torso and pull the wool down tightly.

Use another strand of wool to bind off the **waist** (figure 15). You will need to hold the figure quite tightly so that the proportions turn out correctly and the wool does not slip (see pages 38–39 for notes on proportions). You can use the felting needle to make the waistband a little tighter, attach loose strands of wool, and correct the proportions and shape of the dress (figures 16 to 18). If necessary,

you can also shorten the dress. Finally, don't forget to bend the arms into a natural shape! After completing the basic figure (figure 19), you can add hair and decorative details.

Finishing

Once the hair and details are finished, attach the stand to the figure. To do this, fold back the skirt, fan it out slightly and push the skewer into the firm part of the upper body (figure 20). Then carefully arrange the wool of the skirt around the stand until the stand is not visible any more. Your beautiful fairy is finished.

28

Stable standing figures ✶✶✶

To make stable standing figures, each part of the body needs to be carefully worked with the felting needle. All figures need to be made with care so that they can give many years of pleasure. Each figure has a stable core body cone, made either with Styrofoam or wool. You can decide which suits you better.

Styrofoam cones come in a variety of sizes and are available from craft stores. It is easy to felt over them and they make a quick and simple core body. For a child figure, use a cone 5–6 cm (2–3 in) high, diameter 3–4 cm (1½ in); larger figures need a cone 12–13 cm (5 in) high and 6–7 cm (3 in) diameter.

You can use also leftover bits of wool to make a wool cone and then add a layer of coloured wool. Wind the wool leftovers into a longish 'sausage', then add more wool to the thicker end and needle felt into a correctly shaped and sized cone. It is important to felt the base of the cone as firmly as possible to make a good stable standing surface. You will need approximately 25g (1 oz) of wool for an 'adult' figure.

MATERIALS
- Wool or Styrofoam cone
- Skin-coloured wool
- One pipe cleaner, about 15 cm (6 in)
- Wool for the dress
- Wool for hair

Make the body as described in the Simple standing figures instructions (pages 24–26).

To attach the cone, pull apart the wool at the lower end of the inner body, place it on the cone and very carefully felt in place with the felting needle

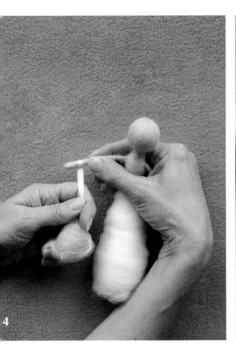

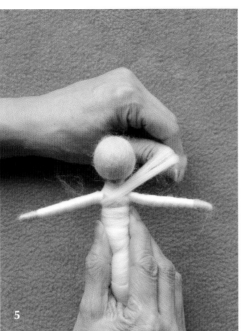

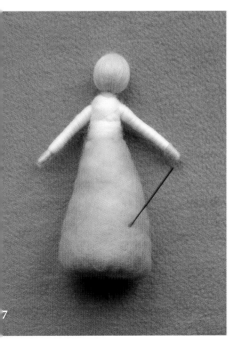

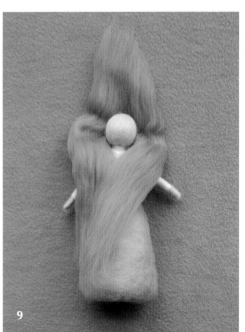

31

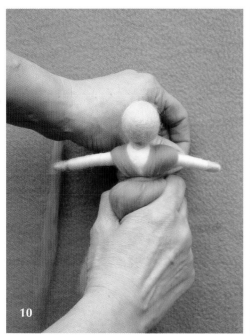

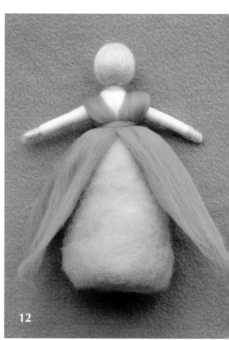

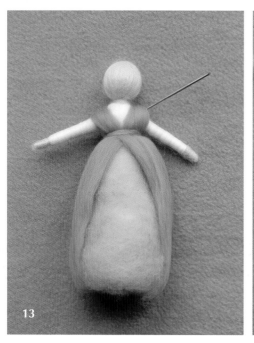

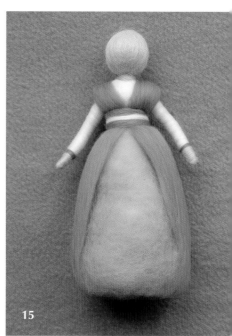

(figures 2 and 3). Keep the proportions in mind. Add a further layer of wool to secure this part. Felt right around the entire Styrofoam cone – make sure you cannot see any Styrofoam through the wool.

Use your imagination to **dress** the figures. Wind around the arms as described in the Simple standing figures instructions for making clothes (see page 26). Arrange the skirt wool around the cone and needle felt in place. Depending on your preference, you can either felt right around the cone, or leave the skirt draped loosely. If you like, you can separate the dress in the centre or divide into several single strands. In general, make the clothes step-by-step and needle felt each step in place. The different finishing details are shown in the instructions for the figures on pages 48–49 onwards. You could make a two-tone skirt, an apron or a dress with petticoats etc. See instructions for the single figures!

To finish, each figure receives a **hairstyle** and possibly **wings**; see the section on wings on page 40. Either felt the wings to the back of the figure with the felting needle, or sew them in place with a needle and thread. When felting in place, make sure not to poke the felting needle right through to the front of the figure.

Making the hair

Hairstyles are a matter of taste! Whether long, put up, plaited, straight, curly, red, blonde, brown or black – experiment to see what suits each figure by laying the wool around the head and then checking the impression it gives. Use the colours of the seasons for inspiration.

This chapter gives examples for felting long or straight hair and curly hair. For details, see individual figure instructions.

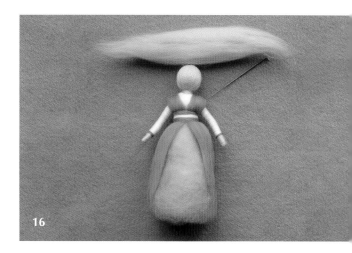

16

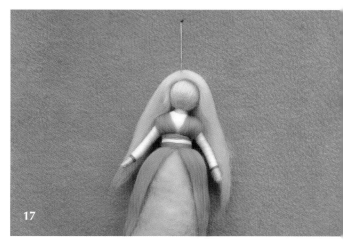

17

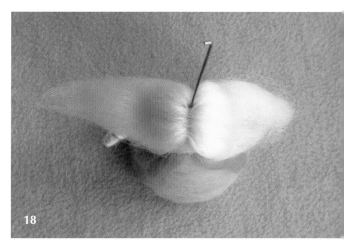

18

19

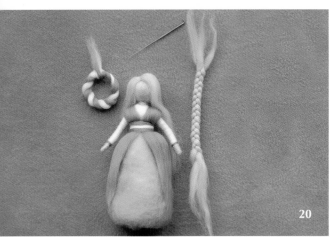

20

Long or straight hair

Always use long wool roving for straight hair.

Place a strand of wool tightly around the head and carefully needle felt in place by poking repeatedly along the parting line (figures 17–19). Make long thick hair for the fairy to start with; you can always pull out wool later to make it thinner or shorter. Make sure you attach the hair to the correct place at the front of the head – the fairy should not have a bald forehead or too small a face. It is equally important to pay attention to the back of the head. Do not felt it too flat. Add more wool if necessary. To finish, carefully poke once around the hairstyle with the felting needle to shape the hair. Be careful not to poke all the way through the head to the face!

You can add wool **plaits** to straight hair. Plait three thin strands of wool, lay them around the head and needle felt in place. You will need to poke repeatedly through the plaits to make them last (figure 20).

You can also make a wreath of two colours of twisted wool. Details are given in the instructions for individual figures.

To make a **bun**, put up the hair and needle felt in place. I like using this hairstyle for making grandmother figures (figure 21).

Occasionally I use strands of silk for hairstyles. This shiny white hair is particularly suited to winter figures. Working with smooth silk fibres is not easy and you will need a lot of patience for satisfactory results. Silk roving can be purchased as slightly yellow tussah silk, white mulberry silk or dyed colours.

21

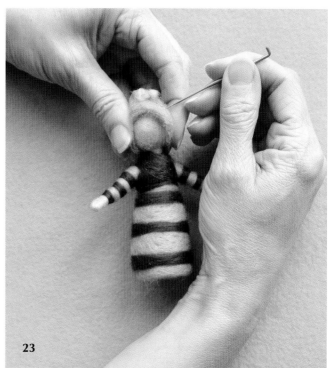

CURLY HAIR

If you want to make curly hair, you will need to sort the wool nubs by hand first. Remove all the dirt, i.e. pieces of grass, burrs, earth, etc. and any pieces that have felted. If necessary, cut out particularly soiled or matted areas with a pair of scissors.

Next, needle felt the curls individually to the head. It is best to start at the back of the head at the neck and work upwards (figure 23). Felt the forehead with special care; the hair should frame the face nicely. Poke the felting needle right around the head to shape the hair.

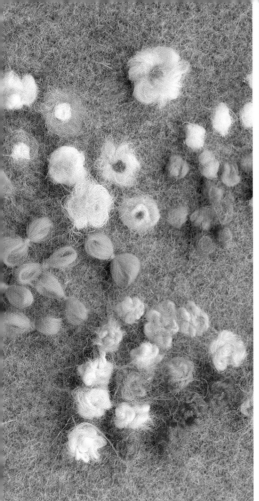

Finishing touches

Adding detail to the figures is probably the most creative part of the work. It is fun thinking about finishing touches and trying them out. The possibilities shown here are suggestions and should help you find your own ideas.

You can use any material, provided it is the correct size and can be felted, sewn or glued in place. How you decorate your figure really depends on your personal taste. Look through your house for glittering stones, stars, tiny buttons, ribbons, beads, silk flowers and leaves, crystals, small candles, feathers or whatever else you can imagine. Just make sure it suits your figure's theme.

If you can't find what you need, make it! You can find different accessories in the individual instructions.

Why doesn't the figure work?

Here are some tips to avoid the most common problems.

The wool

If you choose the wrong wool quality then the results are often unsatisfactory. For larger surfaces, e.g. dresses, wool bat can be more suitable than roving. Winding around wire, on the other hand, is easier to do with the longer fibre roving. Wherever the wool quality is important, I have included it in the instructions. Please take the guidelines into consideration!

The amount of wool

If you use too much wool for the individual steps, the resulting figure may not be well proportioned. Small figures, for example, only need tiny amounts of wool for each layer. This stops the wool slipping and the figure losing shape. It is always better to wind several single layers and add more if necessary.

The head

If the head is not firm enough it will lose its shape more and more while being worked on, and by the time the hair is added it will be completely misshapen. It is even possible the inner ball will slip out, ruining the entire figure. Always make sure the head is firm enough – you can even use a small Styrofoam ball in the beginning. Just make sure the ball is not too hard, or it can break the felting needle.

The arms

Before making a figure it is important to practise the correct technique of winding wool around the pipe cleaner. 'Sausages', huge hands and thin or long arms will destroy the appearance of every figure! It is best to practise winding firmly around several pipe cleaners until you are happy with the results.

Standing surface

If the standing surface of the figures is not firm and even, the figure will keep falling down. Take enough time to work this surface thoroughly with the felting needle.

Proportions

The head size determines the size of the body. A large head makes a figure look childlike and cute, while a smaller head on a long body gives the impression of an adult figure. The head of a male figure can be larger than the head of a female figure.

The sizes given here are intended as a guide for making figures. If you would like to change the size of the figure, the proportions can be maintained if you enlarge or reduce the drawings with a photocopier.

The finished child figures in my examples are about 10 cm (4 in) long. For this size, a head of about 2 cm (¾ in) (without hair) works well. The finished arm length is about 7–8 cm (3 in) from hand to hand.

The adult figures are about 18 cm (7 in) long, with a head diameter of 2½ cm (1 in) and a finished arm length of approximately 13 cm (5 in).

However, it is not possible to make these figures exactly to the millimetre, and in the end everyone has to find their own favourite proportions for their own figures. In the words of Aristotle:

It is the mark of an educated mind to rest satisfied with the degree of precision which the nature of the subject allows and not to seek exactness where only an approximation is possible.

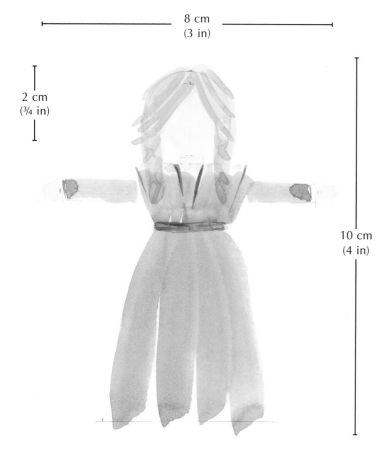

8 cm
(3 in)

2 cm
(¾ in)

10 cm
(4 in)

Child figure

13 cm
(5 in)

2½ cm
(1 in)

18 cm
(7 in)

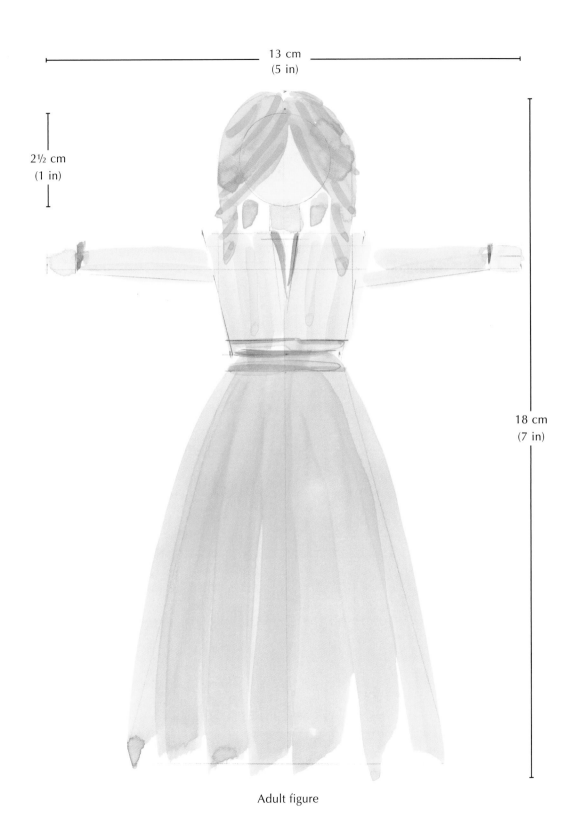

Adult figure

Flying fairy wings

Wet felted butterfly wings

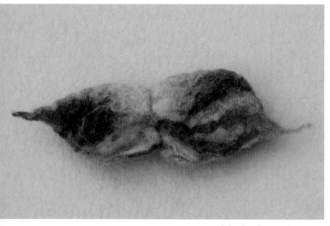

Double-leaf angel wings

Wings

With or without wings? It really depends on the individual figure. While it seems natural to make wings for flying fairies I personally do without wings for the standing figures. On the other hand, I would never make an angel without wings. The shape of the wings should suit the type of figure and its size.

Wool wings

It is quite simple to make wool wings, as they are made out of long fibred wool which is shaped to suit the theme of the figure. Bat is less suitable.

The size of the wings is dependent on the size of the figure. For small figures, 10 cm (4 in) of wool roving is enough. Larger figures can have wings approximately 15–18 cm (6–7 in) long. If the wool does not keep its shape well, you can shorten the wings. Lay the wool on the table, bind it off in the centre and tease it into shape. Needle felt the wings to the back of the figure. Poke the needle into the back repeatedly, but don't poke too far. The final pointy shape of the wings is made by rubbing and twisting the ends of the wings between your fingertips.

You can make a different wing shape by carefully teasing the wool ends apart and fanning them out. Carefully tear off strands of wool that are too long until you end up with an even wing shape.

You can also make multicoloured wings. Place several thin layers of different coloured wool on top of each other. Make sure the wings don't get too thick!

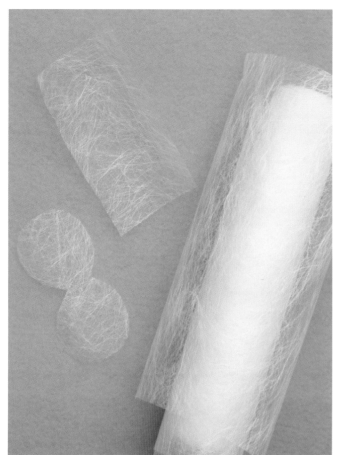
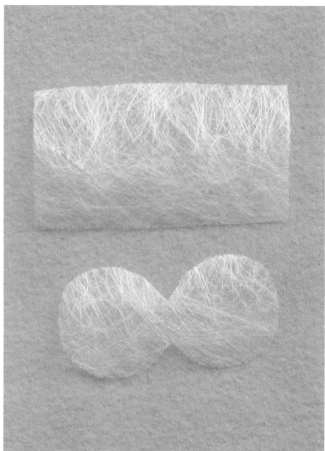

Organza wings

You can make especially light wings using organza. Cut the desired wing shape out of organza and felt to the figure or sew in place with needle and thread. For larger wings, glue a length of wire to the organza to stabilise them. Apply craft glue thinly to one side of the wire, and stick it to the organza. Let it dry well before attaching the wings to the figures.

Tip

Wings can also be wet felted if desired. When planning the size, remember to take wool shrinkage into account.

Colours

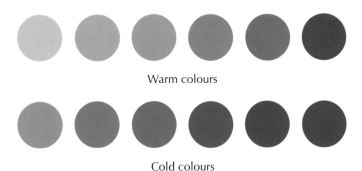

Colour wheel (Johannes Itten)

Warm colours

Cold colours

Bright green, lime green, apple green, birch green, ivy green, fern green, moss green, grass green, jade green, olive green, peppermint green, fir green, spring green…

The range of colours found in nature shows it is not always easy to find the correct shade. It is useful to have some knowledge about colours when working creatively. Here is Johannes Itten's colour circle, which shows the primary and secondary colours.

It is also useful to be able to differentiate between warm and cold colours when deciding which shades to use.

I would like to show how important the correct colour is for each figure, using the example of a summer and winter fairy. The figures on the right are almost identical – apart from a few details. The summer fairy's dress is separated into sun rays, and the icicles on the winter fairy's dress are made in the same way. Only the colours reveal which season the fairy belongs to. The figures depicted in the different chapters will make it easier for beginners to find the colours suited to each season. I have also added the basic colours for each season in the relevant chapters. Naturally there are many shades of each colour – experiment with them. You can mix colours beautifully, like watercolours, by placing thin layers of different coloured wool on top of each other.

Summer fairy

Winter fairy

43

The Seasons

There was a mother
who had four children;
spring, summer,
autumn and winter.
Spring brings flowers,
summer clover,
autumn brings grapes
and winter brings snow.

Folk song from southern Germany

My children learnt this lovely folk song in school. I liked the image so much I immediately wanted to make it with magic wool, with the earth as a queenly mother and the individual seasons as her children.

Mother Earth as an image is present in many cultures. The worship of the life-giving mother figure is deeply rooted in mythology and is as old as humanity itself.

Queen of the seasons ***

MATERIALS

- Skin-coloured wool for the body
- Five pipe cleaners, about 15 cm (6 in)
- Beige, brown and blue wool for the dress
- Brown wool and coloured leftover bits of wool for the cape
- Gold bouillon wire for the head decoration and necklace
- Gold wood stick for the sceptre
- Small transparent beads
- Small fabric leaves (or red craft felt)

INSTRUCTIONS

Follow the instructions for Stable standing figures on page 30 to make the figure. Use either a Styrofoam or wool cone as a standing base.

DETAILS AND DECORATIONS

Wind beige wool around the arms and the cone. Wind a tiny amount of blue wool around the wrists for a contrasting strip. To make the **tunic**, use about 15 cm (6 in) of brown wool roving. Shape the curved tunic hem using a felting needle. Place a small strand of beige wool

around the neck as a collar and felt in place. Then make a bun hairstyle out of brown curly wool.

To make the **cape** you will need a piece of brown wool bat, about 17 x 13 cm (7 x 5 in). Work the bat with the felting needle to make a cape shape. In the centre, felt a circle with the season's colours, approximately 6 cm (3 in) diameter. Add small snowflakes, flowers and autumn leaves to each section. If you cannot obtain small fabric leaves, you can cut them

out of red craft felt or cloth. Once the cape is finished, needle felt it to the back of the figure, leaving a small piece of cape above the neck for the collar.

To finish, wind bouillon wire around the hairstyle several times. Glue a further piece of wire to the shoulder as a necklace (do not pull it apart!). Push the ends under the cape. Attach a bead to the collar and sew the sceptre to the hand. Your queen of the seasons is finished.

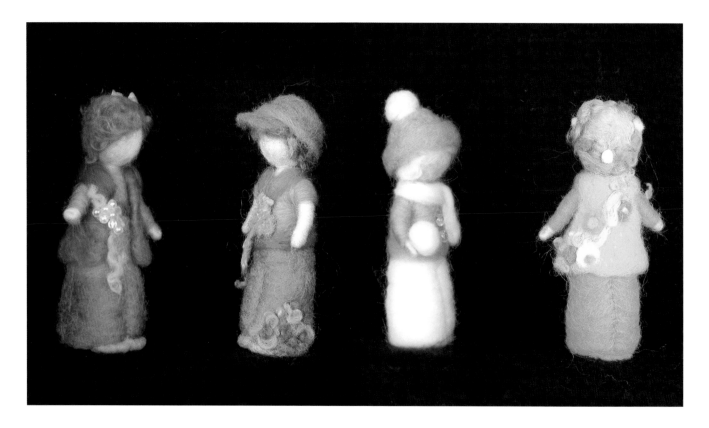

Season's children ★★★

MATERIALS
- White and light blue wool for the winter child
- Light green and yellow wool for the spring child
- Grass green and pinkish red wool for the summer child
- Ochre, orange and yellow-green wool for the autumn child
- Coloured curly nubs for the hair

INSTRUCTIONS
Follow the instructions for Stable standing figures on page 30, following the proportions for a childlike figure. Make the children with a wool cone so you can felt the trouser legs.

WINTER CHILD
Wind light blue wool around the arms and upper body. For the trousers, make a white wool cone and needle felt a groove in the centre to hint at trouser legs. Make a light blue hat on white curly hair. To do this, wind some light blue wool around the head and shape it with the felting needle. Then felt two small, white felt balls. Felt one ball to the top of the hat as a pompom. Glue or sew the second ball to the hand of the winter child – you cannot felt it to the hand due to the wire inside. Place a small strand of white wool around the neck and felt as a scarf.

SPRING CHILD

Wind light green wool around the body, and felt a groove into the centre of the cone to hint at trouser legs. For the waistcoat, use a 7 cm (2–3 in) long piece of wool. Tear it in half and needle felt a small waistcoat to the body. Make a flower wreath and attach it to blond curly hair. To do this, wind a green curl around the head and shape it with the felting needle. Then make several small white, yellow and orange flowers and felt them to the green wreath. Felt further flowers and leaves to the clothes (see page 56–57 for instructions).

SUMMER CHILD

Wind pink-red wool around the arms and upper body. Wind around the body with grass green wool and felt a groove in the centre of the legs, as before. Make a grass green cap on brown curly hair. To do this, wind some grass green wool around the head and shape with the felting needle. Make the peak for the cap separately and then felt it on. Then felt a small green clover leaf to both the jumper and trousers.

AUTUMN CHILD

Wind ochre yellow wool around the body. Make the trousers by winding yellow green wool, changing to green at the bottom, and poke the felting needle along the centre line of the trousers, as before. A 7 cm (2–3 in) long piece of orange wool will be enough for the waistcoat. Pull it in half and needle felt a small waistcoat to the body. Make red curly hair for the autumn child and decorate with a small leaf. Then felt a green wool curl to the waistcoat and add some light green beads as grapes.

This delightful group of figures can accompany you throughout the entire year.

The old and new year ***

The old year must leave to give way to the new year. This event is celebrated through the world with festivals and fireworks and is often a time to look back at the past as well as forward to the future. Everywhere, the new year is greeted with good wishes and blessings.

I have depicted the old year as an elderly woman leaning on her stick. The new year is a child looking into the future with anticipation.

MATERIALS
- Skin-coloured wool for the body
- One pipe cleaner, about 15 cm (6 in)
- Dark pink wool and grey wool for the dress
- Grey curly nubs for the hair
- Small twig

Instructions for the old woman

Follow the instructions for Stable standing figures on page 30. Use the proportions of an adult woman (see figure on page 39). Use a wool cone as the body so you can needle felt her bent posture. This should be done before adding further details. Bend the upper body forwards slightly and bend the head downwards. Make sure the figure can stand securely and does not topple forwards.

Details and decorations

Wind dark pink wool around the arms and cone. To make the top, take a piece of grey wool, about 12 cm (4–5 in) long, and follow the instructions for making clothes on page 26. The top should be short and not reach more than halfway down the skirt. To make the warm shawl, use a piece of grey wool and simply place it over the shoulders. Needle felt in place. Felt several folds into the shawl.

Make a pinned-up hairstyle out of grey curly nubs. Wind the wool around the head and felt it in place right around the head. Pull the ends of wool up at the neck, twist them into a bun and needle felt in place.

Sew a small twig to the old lady's hand so she can stand securely.

Materials for the child

- Skin-coloured wool for the inner body
- One pipe cleaner, about 15 cm (6 in)
- Light blue and pink wool for the dress
- Light yellow wool for the hair
- Pink doll's button

Instructions for the child

Follow the instructions for Stable standing figures on page 30. Use the proportions for a childlike figure.

Details and decorations

Wind light blue wool around the entire body and shape with the felting needle. For the dress, take a piece of light blue wool roving about 13 cm (5 in) long. I added some pink and yellow wool fibres to the blue wool. Sew a small doll's button to the belt for decoration.

To make the hair, felt some pale yellow wool to the centre of the head and plait it into two.

Bend the small body sideways and arrange the figures to make the new year peek out behind the old year with anticipation.

Spring

The colours of spring are white, green, light purple and pink and bright yellow. In spring, all the colours should be fresh and clean.

Spring fairy **

The spring fairy brings the first green and delicate flowers, which is why I am fond of depicting her with a basket filled with blossoms. She makes me think of nature awakening to new life in spring. I like to make the main fairies of the seasons slightly larger than the rest of the figures to demonstrate their importance. 1–2 cm (½ in) taller is sufficient to achieve the desired effect.

This fairy needs a particularly voluminous skirt to cover the wood stand. See the collection of ideas on page 107 for additional spring fairies.

See the collection of ideas on page 107 for additional spring fairies.

MATERIALS
- Skin-coloured wool for the body
- One pipe cleaner, about 15 cm (6 in)
- White, light pink and light green wool roving
- Small fluffs of wool in different pink shades
- Light yellow wool for hair
- Small basket

54

INSTRUCTIONS

Follow the instructions for Simple standing figures on page 22. Use the proportions for an adult figure (see figure on page 39) and give her a wooden stand.

DETAILS AND DECORATIONS

Wind white wool around the arms and upper body, then wind fluffs of green wool crosswise around the lower sleeves.

Choose a piece of wool roving and if necessary add some wool to the skirt to ensure the stand is completely covered. (I added some white wool to this figure.) To make the top of her dress, take a piece of light pink wool about 30 cm (12 in) long and follow the instructions for making clothes on page 26. Felt the top of the dress lightly to the top of the figure. Spread the wool of the skirt evenly around the figure and shorten the lower edge to the required dress length.

Then use smooth yellow wool to make the hair. Add lots of small wool flowers and green vines for decoration. Make these individually (see the instructions overleaf) and felt them to the head. Decorate the fairy's belt with more flowers and vines.

Fill the basket with small wool flowers and leaves.

You could also make a spring fairy with slightly

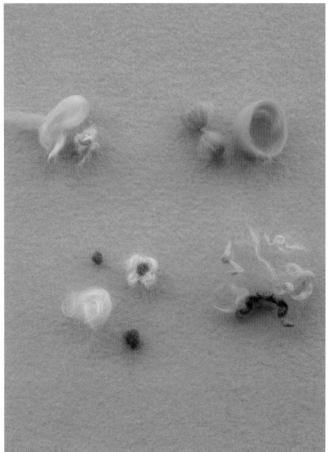

Clockwise from top left: rose, double leaf, vine, two-tone flower

different colours. Make a skirt with bright pink, light pink and white wool. Place the different colours on top of each other in layers; first bright pink wool, then a thin layer of light pink wool and finally a thin layer of white wool. Carefully smooth over the fibres. Felt this skirt to the upper body of the figure. Then add the green top and the flower decorations as described above.

Wool flowers and leaves

You will only need tiny amounts of wool in the desired colour for making flowers and leaves.

ROSES

Turn a tiny amount of wool fibres between your fingers until the wool yarn starts to twist itself. Fix the shape by poking into it several times with the felting needle.

Two-tone flowers

Rub a small amount of wool fibres between your fingers until they turn into a fluffy ball. Take an even smaller amount of wool in a different colour to make a second, smaller ball. Place the smaller wool ball on top of the larger ball and fix in the centre with the felting needle. For larger flowers you can create single petals with the felting needle.

Double leaves

Wind a very small amount of green wool fibres several times around a 2½ cm (1 in) cardboard strip, slip the wool off and tie it off in the centre with a tiny amount of wool. You can attach the flowers described above to these double leaves with a few pokes of the felting needle.

Vines

Use green curly wool to make the vines. If necessary, shorten them to the desired length and fasten in place with the felting needle.

Dancing spring children ***

The small spring children have made flower wreaths and are dancing 'ring a ring o' roses' on the meadow to celebrate the spring. Naturally, you can add more dancers to this group of children.

- Skin-coloured wool for the inner body
- Pipe cleaners, one for each child, about 15 cm (6 in)
- Blue, orange, yellow and green wool
- Brown curly nubs for the smallest child
- Light yellow wool roving for the hair of the larger child

INSTRUCTIONS

Follow the instructions for Stable standing figures on page 30. Use the proportions for a childlike figure (see figure on page 38). It is best to make the very small child with a wool cone; larger children can be made with a wool or Styrofoam cone as a body core.

DETAILS AND DECORATIONS

The children depicted only differ in colour, size and hairstyle, so I will only describe the larger (blue) girl; the smaller girl is made with orange wool. Wind around the body with blue wool. To make the dress, take a length of blue wool about 13 cm (5 in). Pull it around the cone and felt in place with the felting needle. Make a flower wreath on blonde hair for the spring child. To do this, wind a length of green curly wool around the head and shape it with the felting needle.

To finish, felt several small yellow flowers to the dress and wreath and felt a short green curl as a belt decoration to the front of the dress.

Tree flower fairy ***

A tree in full bloom is a beautiful sight. Tree fairies or nymphs are inseparable from their trees; they help them to grow and flourish and protect them. Due to this close connection, when a tree is chopped down or dies, so does the tree nymph.

MATERIALS
- Skin-coloured wool for the inner body
- One pipe cleaner, about 15 cm (6 in)
- Red-pink, light pink, green and brown wool for the dress
- Dark brown wool roving for the hair
- Small twig
- Sewing thread and sewing needle

INSTRUCTIONS

Follow the instructions for Stable standing figures on page 30 to make the fairy. Use the proportions for an adult figure (see figure on page 39), with a wool or Styrofoam cone as a body core.

DETAILS AND DECORATIONS

Wind light pink wool around the arms and upper body. Add a green strip of wool as a colour contrast around the wrists. Wind pink-red wool completely around the cone to make the **skirt**. To make the top of the dress, take a piece of light pink wool roving approximately 30 cm (12 in) long and follow the instructions for making clothes on page 26. Felt it lightly in place. Pull the wool apart at the front of the dress. Place a small strand of brown wool vertically along the edge of the dress and felt in place. Then make the **hair** out of dark brown wool roving. Decorate with a hair band made out of green wool.

Make small wool flowers on a double leaf for the belt and hair band and felt them in place (see Wool flowers and leaves on page 57). Then make additional flowers and attach them to the twig with a wool fibre or sewing thread.

Sew the twig to the hand – and your pretty tree flower fairy is finished.

Easter fairy ***

The term *Easter* may derive from *Ostara*, the name of a pre-Christian goddess who is connected to spring rituals. These are instructions for making an Easter fairy with symbols such as the Celtic 'egg' shape on her skirt.

MATERIALS
- Skin-coloured wool for the body
- One pipe cleaner, about 15 cm (6 in)
- White, yellow-green and bright green wool for the dress
- Light yellow wool for the hair

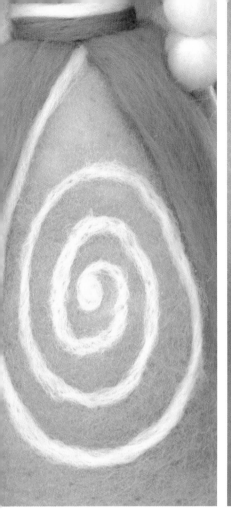 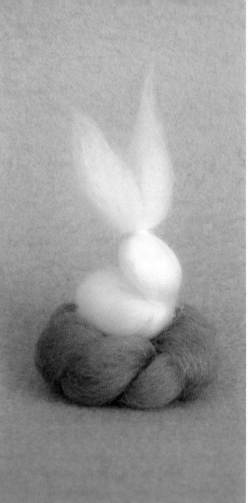 

INSTRUCTIONS

Follow the instructions for Stable standing figures on page 30. Use the proportions for an adult figure (see figure on page 39). If you make a wool cone, make it very stable so you can felt the spiral on the dress later.

DETAILS AND DECORATIONS

Wind white wool around the arms and upper body; wind an additional strip of green wool around the wrist as a cuff. Wind yellow-green wool around the skirt cone. Take a piece of bright green wool about 30 cm (12 in) long to make the top of the dress and follow the instructions for making clothes on page 26. Pull it apart at the front and felt lightly in place. Wind this fairy's waist higher and use two colours. To make the spiral, twist white wool fibres into a thin wool strand and felt them on, section by section.

Make the hair out of light yellow wool and add a twisted hair band made out of green and white wool. A small white rabbit (see page 19) completes the picture of the beautiful Easter fairy.

Easter girls ***

Two little girls looking for Easter eggs are a sweet addition to an Easter table. If you like, you could also make two little boys; see instructions for children on page 30.

see instructions for children on page 30.

MATERIALS
- Skin-coloured wool for the body
- Pipe cleaners, one for each child, about 15 cm (6 in)
- Bright pink, light pink, ochre yellow and green wool
- Green wool nubs
- Coloured wool nubs for the hair
- Small fabric flowers (or felt/wool flowers)
- Small basket and small coloured wood eggs

INSTRUCTIONS

Follow the instructions for Stable standing figures on page 30. Use the proportions for a childlike figure (see figure on page 38). It is best to make very small children with a wool cone; larger children can be made either with a wool or a Styrofoam cone.

DETAILS AND DECORATIONS

The children depicted here differ only in size, colour and hairstyles, so I will describe the smaller (pink) girl. Make the larger girl with ochre yellow wool.

This figure shows the effect of different types of wool. The bottom layer is carefully wound with coarse, plant dyed wool. The upper layer is made with smooth wool roving.

Wind bright pink wool around the body. A piece of light pink wool about 15 cm (6 in) long will suffice for the upper layer of the **dress**. Pull it right over the cone and needle felt in place.

Make a **flower wreath** for spring child's curly blonde hair. Simply twist the hair into a bun and needle felt in place. To make the wreath, needle felt a length of light green wool nub to the hair.

To finish, glue several small pink flowers to the dress and hair wreath and felt a green curl to the front of the dress as a decoration.

To make the Easter nests, wind a small strand of green wool into a circle; if necessary, needle felt into a nest shape. Fill with little wooden eggs.

Easter bunny *

This is the easy way to make lovely fluffy Easter bunnies. I have made these bunnies hundreds of times with children – even with those with no experience of wool and felting – and they always look great.

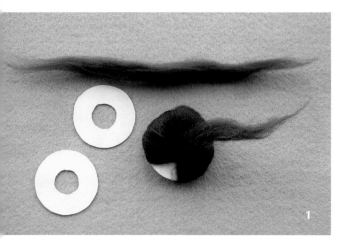

MATERIALS
- White, brown, beige, green or black wool roving
- Strong cotton yarn
- Cardboard
- Compass
- Scissors

INSTRUCTIONS
Draw two circles on the cardboard, each with a larger outer circle of 6 cm (3 in) and a smaller inner circumference of 2½–3 cm (1–1½ in). Cut them out with scissors. Place the cardboard rings on top of each other – this is the template for the pompom. Take a length of roving and wind around the cardboard rings. Repeat this process until the inner hole is very small (figure 1).

Now cut the wool around the outer edge of the rings. Take a double length of cotton yarn and wrap it between the cardboard rings. Pull together as tightly as possible and knot the ends (figure 2). Remove the cardboard rings (if necessary, cut them so you can pull them out). You will have a fluffy pompom. Cut the threads hanging out. Trim the ball into an egg shape with scissors.

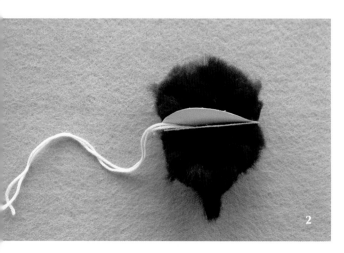

Felt a ridge right around one end to make the head.

To make the rabbit ears, felt a piece of wool about 10 cm (4 in) long to the centre of the head (figures 3 and 4) – and the Easter bunny is finished.

You can use a larger cardboard circle to make larger bunnies. For example, try an 8 cm (3 in) outer circumference and 4 cm (1½ in) circumference for the inner circle.

Summer

Strong summer colours come out in blooming flower beds, ripe vegetables and fruits. Bright yellows, blues, greens and reds are excellent colours for this season.

Summer fairy ***

This lovely fairy reminds me of bright sunshine.
You can also make a beautiful summer fairy with
summer flowers; there is a description of a fairy
like this in the More Ideas section at the end of
the book.

MATERIALS
- Skin-coloured wool for the body
- One pipe cleaner, about 15 cm (6 in)
- Different shades of yellow wool
- Small metal sun ornaments (you can make
  your own out of metal foil)
- Small gold beads

Instructions

Follow the instructions for Stable standing figures on page 30. Use the proportions for an adult figure (see figure on page 39), with a wool or Styrofoam cone as the body core.

Details and decorations

Wind yellow wool around the arms and the upper body. Wind yellow wool completely around the cone. Take a piece of yellow wool about 30 cm (12 in) long for the top of the dress and follow the instructions for making clothes on page 26. Felt lightly in place. Distribute the skirt wool evenly around the figure and gently tear the lower edges to fit the length of the dress (do not cut!). Now divide the skirt wool into equal parts to make 'sun rays' and felt them very lightly in place. Make a hairstyle for the fairy out of yellow wool and add a gold metal crown.

Glue extra beads and pearls to the belt and skirt. The amount you use depends on your taste. If you like, you can make a gold coloured stick topped with an ornamental sun too.

Sun decorations

You can find different types of sun decoration, like large sun-shaped sequins, in craft stores. You can also use stamps – stamp and cut out the suns and glue them in place. Little metal ornaments from jewellery shops can also be used. Just make sure you have the correct proportions!

Bee queen ***

This busy bee queen is buzzing over a flowering meadow, with her worker bees collecting nectar. She is a perfect celebration of summer.

MATERIALS

- Skin-coloured wool for the body
- One pipe cleaner, about 15 cm (6 in)
- Dark brown and yellow wool
- White long-fibred wool roving for wings
- Dark brown wool roving for hair
- Dark brown flower pistil for the feelers (or use wire with beads)
- Small metal crown

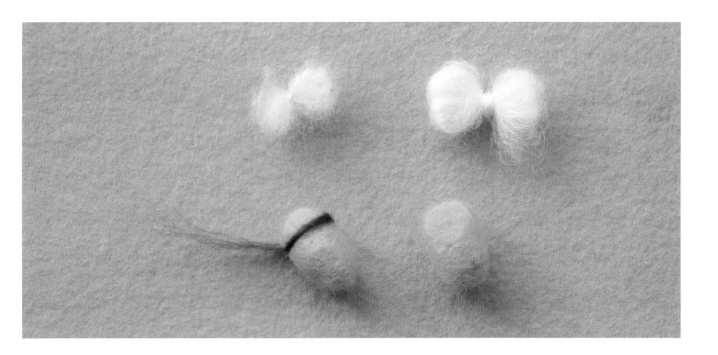

INSTRUCTIONS

Follow the instructions for Stable standing figures on page 30. Use the proportions for an adult figure (see figure on page 39), with a wool or Styrofoam cone as a body core.

DETAILS AND DECORATIONS

Wind wool completely around the arms and cone, alternating brown and yellow to make stripes. Needle felt the layers in place.

Lay a piece of brown wool about 10 cm (4 in) long around the neck and felt it on as a bulky collar. Use a flower pistil for making the feelers. Bend it in half and glue or sew to the head. Then make the hair out of brown wool. Lay the wool around the head and needle felt in place. Felt two small wool balls to make buns to the left and right of the head. Sew or glue the small crown to the head.

Make **wings** for the bee queen using white wool roving (see Wool wings on page 40). Felt them to the back of the figure.

The queen is holding is a **small bee** in her hand. The tiny bee is made out of a small piece of yellow wool. Make a yellow egg-shaped bead and wind tiny fluffs of brown wool around it to make stripes (see figure above). Make the wings following the instructions on page 40 and felt to the top of the bee. You can also hang up small bees with a thread to let them fly around the bee queen.

Bee children ***

Here is a selection of little bee children you can make to accompany the bee queen.

MATERIALS
- Skin-coloured wool for the body
- Pipe cleaners, one for each bee child, about 15 cm (6 in)
- Dark brown and yellow wool
- Yellow curly wool
- Dark brown flower pistil for the feelers (or use wire with beads)
- White organza for the wings

INSTRUCTIONS

Follow the instructions for Stable standing figures on page 30. Use the proportions for a childlike figure (see figure on page 39). It is best to make very small bee children with a wool cone. Larger children can be made either with a wool or a Styrofoam cone as the body core.

DETAILS AND DECORATIONS

Wind yellow wool around the arms and cone. Then felt stripes with brown wool (figures 1 to 3 overleaf). Needle felt the wool layers in place.

Bend the flower pistil in half and attach it to the head with needle and thread or a drop of glue. Felt yellow curly hair (figures 4 to 6 overleaf). Cut out the organza for the wings (see pattern) and felt to the back of the bees (figures 7 to 8 overleaf).

Once you have finished the basic bee child, decide what your bees should be doing. In the examples shown here, one has flower pollen, the next is carrying honey in a bowl, and one bee child has spilled some honey! Busy bees could be filling honeycombs.

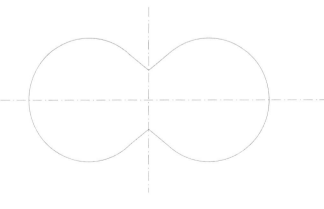

Pattern for organza wings

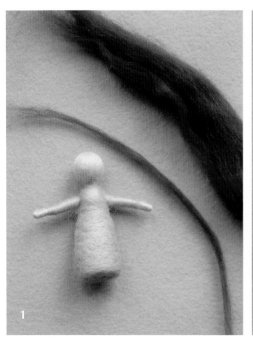

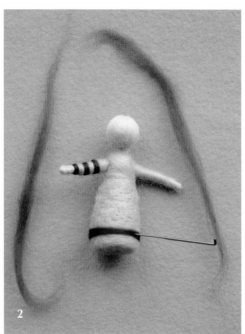

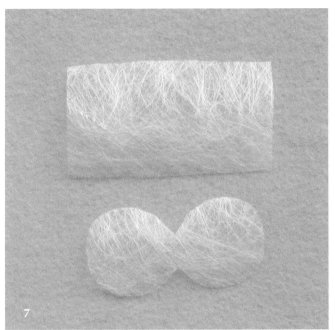

BASKET WITH FLOWER POLLEN

Baskets like this are available from doll's house suppliers. Alternatively, you could crochet a small basket out of raffia ribbon. Fill the basket with small yellow felt balls. To make the balls, rub a few fluffs of yellow wool between your fingers. Glue or sew a felt ball to a bee child's hand.

BOWL WITH HONEY

Use acorns to make bowls. If you can collect them from different oak trees, you will find varying shapes and sizes. I always collect a store of acorns for the year in autumn. Leave them to dry and, depending on your taste, paint them or leave them natural. Fill these acorn cups with melted beeswax and glue to the hand of a bee child.

Large bee *

This fat bee is very simple to make. The example shown here is a large bee, about 12 cm (4–5 in) long. You can make even larger bees, or much smaller ones, in exactly the same way; just change the proportions.

MATERIALS
- Dark brown and yellow wool roving
- Strong cotton yarn
- Cardboard
- Compass
- Scissors
- Brown chenille wire, about 12–14 cm (5–6in)
- White organza for the wings
- Sewing thread and needle

INSTRUCTIONS
To make a bee about 12 cm (4–5 in) long, draw two circles on the cardboard, each with an outer circumference of 12 cm (4–5 in) and a smaller inner circumference of 6 cm (2½ in). Cut them out with a pair of scissors (see figure 1 on page 66). Place the rings on top of each other – this is the template for the pompom.

Take a length of dark brown wool roving and wind around the cardboard rings. Repeat this process until the double ring is completely covered in a layer of brown wool. Then add a layer of yellow wool. Repeat this process, alternating brown and yellow layers, until there is only a very small hole in the centre.

Cut the wool right around the edge of the ring with a pair of scissors. Take a length of cotton thread and wrap it around the pompom between the two cardboard rings. Pull together as tightly as possible and knot. Remove the cardboard ring; cut it if necessary. Your fluffy pompom is finished. If necessary, trim the thread hanging out and cut the ball into a brown and yellow striped egg with the scissors. Bend the chenille wire in half, bend back the ends and sew to the head of the bee as feelers.

Cut out the organza for the wings (see pattern on page 75) and sew to the back of the bee. Attach a thread for hanging up and the fat bee can fly!

Summer flowers in a pot *

The flowers shown here are small sunflowers, daisies and zinnias. With a simple change of petal colour and shape you can easily make a variety of other flower children. Flowers from other seasons (for example, a red Christmas flower) are also pretty.

MATERIALS

- Skin-coloured and natural brown wool
- Yellow or brown wool for the hair
- Craft felt in the colours needed for the flowers
- Sewing needle and sewing thread
- Small clay pot, circumference 5 cm (2 in)

INSTRUCTIONS FOR FLOWERS
See Simple Figures on page 22.

DETAILS AND DECORATIONS
After completing the basic steps, make different small flower children instead of shoots. To do this, leave out step 2 of the basic instructions and cut the petals of small sunflowers, daisies or zinnias out of craft felt (see pattern overleaf). Fold the petals in half and sew or felt them in a wreath around the head. Cover the 'bald spot' with hair in suitable colours.

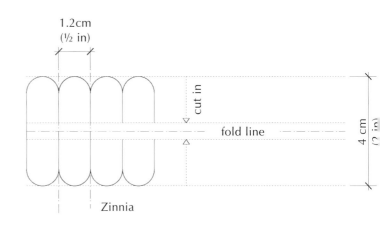

1.2cm
(½ in)

cut in

fold line

4 cm
(2 in)

Zinnia

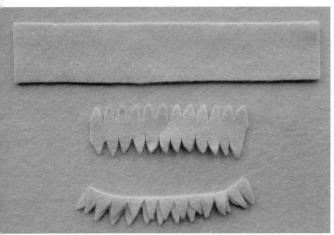

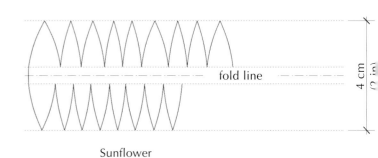

fold line

4 cm
(2 in)

Sunflower

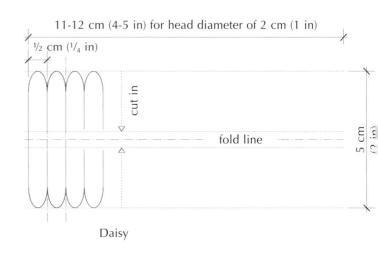

11-12 cm (4-5 in) for head diameter of 2 cm (1 in)

½ cm (¼ in)

cut in

fold line

5 cm
(2 in)

Daisy

Water nymphs and mermaids

Water nymphs and mermaids live in small ponds and large lakes, rushing rivers and bubbling brooks, frothing fountains and cool springs. And, of course, their songs can always be heard in the roaring waves of the sea…

Who would be
A mermaid fair
Singing alone,
Combing her hair
Under the sea
In a golden curl
With a comb of pearl,
On a throne?

Tennyson, *The Mermaid*

Large mermaid **

Mermaids are said to lure sailors to their death in deep waters with their beauty and song. Many children will be familiar with Hans Christian Andersen's story of the little mermaid who enchanted a handsome prince with her song.

MATERIALS
- Skin-coloured wool for the body
- Three pipe cleaners, about 15 cm (6 in)
- Blue, green and turquoise wool
- Silk fibres in suitable colours, if desired
- Turquoise wool nubs for the hair
- Small and large beads
- Large shell

INSTRUCTIONS

The instructions for making the mermaid with her tail are slightly different to other figures. To make the upper body, see the Simple standing figures on page 22. Before winding skin-coloured wool around the arm, hang two further pipe cleaners over the shoulders for the tail. Make the mermaid according to the proportions of an adult (see figure on page 39) with a tail.

DETAILS AND DECORATIONS

Wind skin-coloured wool completely around the arms and upper body. Make sure the arms are a natural thickness as the mermaid's arms are exposed. Then pull over a dress of skin-coloured wool. Needle felt the upper body, pushing the wool layers together.

To make the **tail**, wind blue, green and turquoise wool all the way down the body. Felt the tail fin separately and then needle felt to the tail. Needle felt the whole tail into shape. You can add some silk fibres to make a shiny sheen.

Then make a hairstyle out of turquoise wool nubs. Needle felt each curl individually to the head.

Decorate the mermaid with small shells and a tiny pearl necklace and then place her in a large shell.

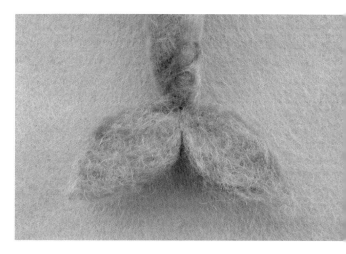

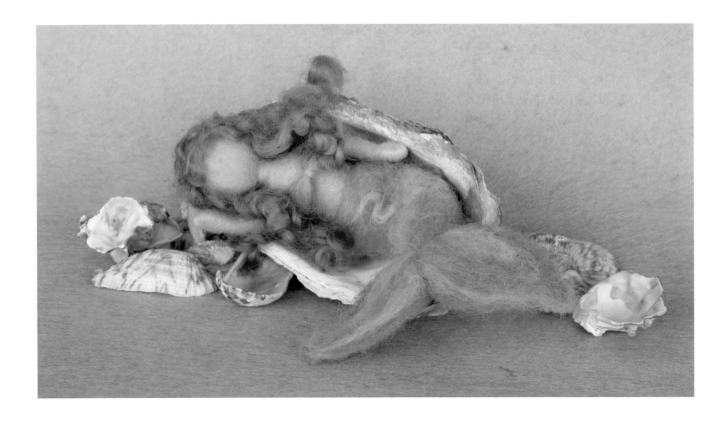

Small mermaid **

This little mermaid is sleeping peacefully in her oyster shell deep under the sea.

MATERIALS
- Skin-coloured wool for the body
- Three pipe cleaners, about 15 cm (6 in)
- Blue, green and turquoise wool
- Silk fibres in suitable colours, if desired
- Red wool nubs for the hair
- Large shell

INSTRUCTIONS
Follow the instructions for the large mermaid, but make the small mermaid according to the proportions of a child (see figure on page 38). Shorten the pipe cleaners for the tail accordingly.

See the More Ideas at the back of the book for further ideas for making mermaids. You can make an attractive mobile for mermaid fans by adding several colourful wool fish.

Tip

Often you can find large shells in home decor stores. Alternatively, you could collect them yourself on the beach or ask a fishmonger or restaurant for empty shells.

Water nymph ***

Water nymphs live in or around water, but do not have a tail. They are similar in appearance to humans and they guard, protect and nurture their territory. In the example shown here, the water nymph is collecting water in a small shell. Her clothes complement the shell's colours.

MATERIALS

- Skin-coloured wool for the body
- One pipe cleaner, about 15 cm (6 in)
- Green or violet wool for the dress
- Light blond wool nubs for the hair
- Small and large glass beads
- Small fabric flowers
- Small shells
- Rhinestone glue or fabric glue

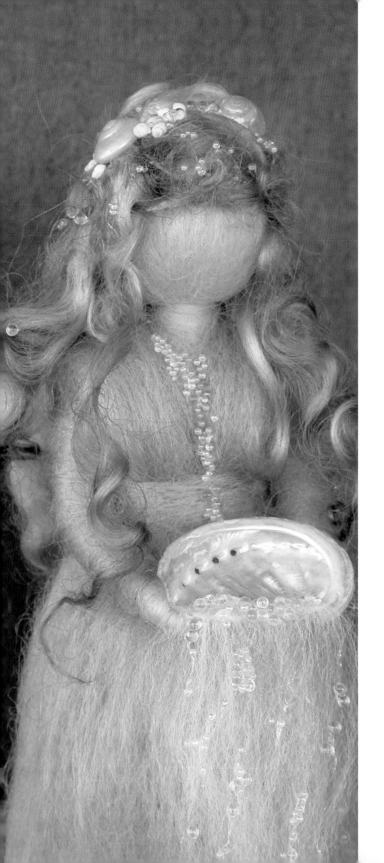

Instructions

Follow the instructions for Stable standing figures on page 30, with a wool or Styrofoam cone as a body core.

Details and decorations for the green water nymph

Wind green wool around the arms and upper body. Wind green wool completely around the skirt cone. To make the top of the dress, take a piece of green wool about 30 cm (12 in) long and follow the instructions for making clothes on page 26. Needle felt the entire dress.

Make the hair out of pale yellow wool nubs. Place a twist of green wool on the head as a hair band. Glue small white textile flowers to the dress and hair band. Alternatively, felt them in place with some light green and cream wool fluffs.

Use a spiral shell as a water scoop. Glue some long white wool fibres to the edge of the shell to depict flowing water. Add small beads to the water.

Glue the shell to the hand and lower arm of the nymph.

Details and decorations for the violet water nymph

Wind plant dyed light violet wool completely around this nymph. Make the hair with violet nubs. Carefully needle felt each curl in place.

Glue lots of small shells and shiny glass beads to the nymph's dress and hair. How many you use is entirely up to you. This fairy is carrying a small shimmering abalone shell; its mother-of-pearl sheen echoes the colour of this nymph.

Autumn

Autumn colours are warm and shimmering. Red gold, gold green, orange brown, ochre yellow, dark red and aubergine purple are the colours of autumn. They all merge together like beautiful autumn leaves.

Autumn fairy **

In autumn the fruits of the earth are harvested,
so I have made this fairy a dark burgundy red,
in celebration of the autumnal grape harvest.
See More Ideas at the back of the book for more
examples of yellow, orange and green autumn
fairies.

MATERIALS
- Skin-coloured wool for the body
- One pipe cleaner, about 15 cm (6 in)
- Pink and wine-red wool for the dress
- Dark brown wool for the hair
- Green silk fibres
- Small glass beads in different sizes
- Decorative moss
- Rhinestone glue or craft glue

INSTRUCTIONS

Follow the instructions for Simple standing figures on page 24. Use the proportions for an adult figure (see figure on page 39). This fairy has a wooden stand as a body core.

DETAILS AND DECORATIONS

Wind pink wool completely around the arms and upper body, then wind green silk fibres crosswise around the arms.

Use a strand of roving for the fairy and if necessary, add more wool to the skirt to cover the wooden stand completely. For the top of the **dress**, take a piece of wine red wool about 30 cm (12 in) long, and follow the instructions for making clothes on page 26. Felt the top of the dress lightly to the upper body.

Spread the skirt around the figure evenly, and shorten it to your desired length. Decorate the fairy's dress with silk fibres, decorative moss strands, small wool flowers and glass beads. Felt the wool and silk to the dress and glue the moss

and beads in place with tiny drops of craft glue or rhinestone glue.

Make the **hairstyle** using dark brown wool roving and add a hair wreath made out of small flowers, green tendrils and beads. Make each flower individually (see instructions on page 56–57) and felt to the head.

If you want, you can make a basket full of harvest products. Rub different coloured small tufts of wool between your fingers and work with the felting needle until you have made small apples, pears or pumpkins.

Tip

You can make beautiful shiny effects with fine coloured silk fibres. If you do not have any silk, you can use green wool nubs instead.

Shepherd ***

This shepherd is herding the sheep after a summer in the fields, but shepherds also suit other seasons – at Christmas time they are found in every nativity scene. The shepherd in this example is made entirely out of natural coloured wool. You can also use dyed wool, so long as you do not choose colours that are too bright.

- Skin-coloured wool for the body
- One pipe cleaner, about 15 cm (6 in)
- Natural brown and beige wool
- Brown uncarded wool for the cape and hat
- Grey wool for the hair and beard
- Small twig for the staff

Instructions

Follow the instructions for Stable standing figures on page 30. Use the proportions for an adult figure (see figure on page 39), with a wool or Styrofoam cone as the body core. Make a slightly larger head to indicate a male figure.

Details and decorations

Wind natural brown wool completely around the arms and cone. To make the cape, use uncarded wool and felt it into a fleece texture, to create the impression of a sheepskin over one shoulder. You can also use a piece of wool roving to make the cape. Take a piece of wool about 18 cm (7 in) long and follow the instructions for making clothes on page 26. Felt lightly in place.

Make a large beard and hair out of natural grey wool. As this figure has a hat, you can needle felt the hair in a ring around the head.

To make the hat, felt a circle using the same wool as the cape. Place it directly on to the head and felt in place with the felting needle. Twist some beige wool into a cord and needle felt in place as a band around the hat.

To finish, sew the twig to the hand and the shepherd is ready to take care of his flock.

To make the **sheep** lying down, see page 19. Depending on the length of the wire, you can make large sheep or small lambs.

Mother Earth ***

This figure is based on the drawings in the children's book *The Story of the Root Children* by Sibylle von Olfers. She is depicted as an old woman with an apron and a knitting basket. There is also a figure of mother earth as a celtic fairy in the collection of suggestions at the back of this book – be inspired to create your own ideas!

MATERIALS

- Skin-coloured wool for the body
- One pipe cleaner, about 15 cm (6 in)
- Beige and brown wool for the dress
- Grey wool for the hair
- Small willow basket
- Two pins

INSTRUCTIONS

Follow the instructions for Stable standing figures on page 30. Use the proportions for an adult figure (see figure on page 39), with a wool or Styrofoam cone as a body core.

DETAILS AND DECORATIONS

Wind brown wool completely around the arms and the cone. Take a piece of beige wool about 30 cm (12 in) long for the top of the dress and follow the instructions for making clothes on page 26. The top of the dress is Mother Earth's apron. To make it, felt the lower edge of the apron approximately 2 cm (¾ in) above the standing base.

Make the hair for Mother Earth out of grey wool. Wind the wool smoothly around the head and felt in place. Pull the wool up at the neck and twist it up into a bun, then needle felt in place.

Fill the small basket with colourful wool balls and push two pins into it as knitting needles.

Root Children ***

MATERIALS

- Skin-coloured wool for the body
- Pipe cleaners, one for each child, about 15 cm (6 in)
- Different shades of brown wool
- Brown wool nubs for hair

INSTRUCTIONS

Follow the instructions for Stable standing figures on page 30. Use the proportions for a childlike figure (see figure on page 38). Vary the sizes – you can make a little baby in a walnut shell, and a much a bigger child. It is best to make very small children with a wool cone as the inner core.

DETAILS AND DECORATIONS

Wind brown wool around the whole body and use the felting needle to shape the child. To make the hair, felt nubs to the head, leaving a few curls standing up like roots. If you have different shades of brown nubs, make the children with different colours for a bit of variety.

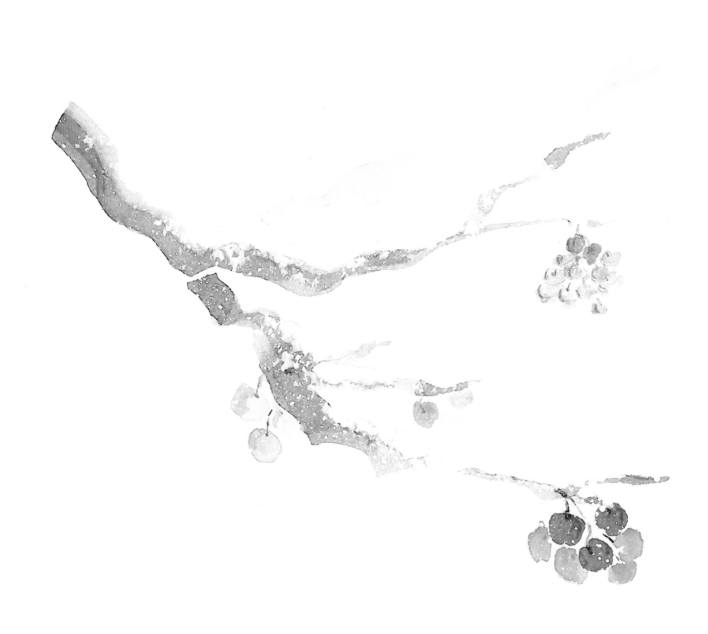

Winter

The colours of winter are as crisp and clear as the wintry air. White, light blue, turquoise, grey, violet – and these colours look even better if they are covered in glittering frost!

Winter fairy ***

The winter fairy brings ice and snow, but she also represents a time of peace. Nature is covered by a layer of snow and sleeps under its white blanket until spring arrives again.

MATERIALS

- Skin-coloured wool for the body
- One pipe cleaner, about 15 cm (6 in)
- White and light blue wool
- White silk for the hair
- Small white beads
- Hat needle topped with a white bead

Instructions

Follow the instructions for Stable standing figures on page 30. Use the proportions for an adult figure (see figure on page 39), with a wool or Styrofoam cone as a body core.

Details and decorations

Wind white wool around the arms and upper body. Wind light blue around the skirt cone. To make the top of the **dress**, take about 30 cm (12 in) of white wool and pull it over the head, following the instructions for making clothes on page 26. Felt it lightly to the upper body. While doing this, evenly spread the skirt wool around the figure and gently tear the bottom to match the skirt length (do not cut the wool!). Divide the skirt into equal parts to make icicles, and lightly felt them to the dress.

Make the **hair** out of white silk. Add a decorative hair band of small white beads. String the beads along a thread and sew them in place. Sew or glue further small white beads to the belt and the skirt.

Use the hat needle topped with a large white bead and three smaller beads below to make the **sceptre**. Push the needle through the figure's hand and remove the sharp tip with a pair of pliers.

Alternatively, you can decorate the winter fairy with rhinestones, to make her glitter like freshly fallen snow!

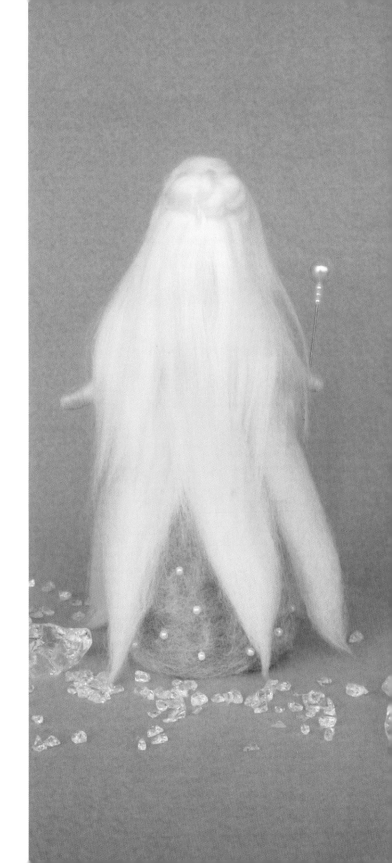

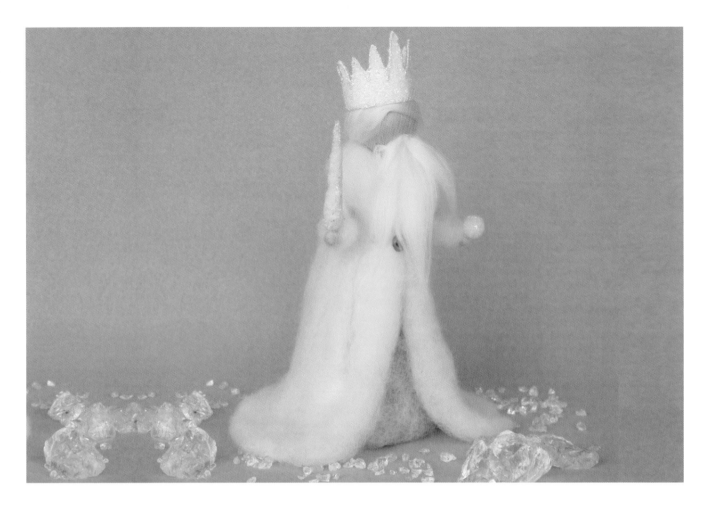

King Winter ***

King Winter transforms the earth into a glittering winter wonderland. He rules a frosty realm and brings icy temperatures and bitterly cold days and nights. His rule starts with the shortest day and longest night of the year.

MATERIALS

- Skin-coloured wool for the body
- One pipe cleaner, about 15 cm (6 in)
- White and light blue wool
- White silk for the hair
- Light blue rhinestone
- One large white bead
- White glitter and craft glue
- White cardboard or paper for the crown and sceptre

INSTRUCTIONS

Follow the instructions for Stable standing figures on page 30. Use the proportions for an adult figure (see figure on page 39), but make a larger wool ball for the head. The King can be slightly larger than the female figures.

DETAILS AND DECORATIONS

Wind white wool around the arms and upper body. Wind a little extra around the lower arms to make the sleeve shape depicted. Wind light blue wool around the skirt.

To make the **cloak**, take a piece of white wool bat about 15 x 29 cm (6 x 12 in) and felt it lightly over a sponge – this is quickest if you use a needle holder with several felting needles. Make two small holes at the shoulder for the arms and put it on like a cloak. Fold down the upper edge to make a large collar and felt in place.

Now spread the cloak evenly around the figure and needle felt in place. Felt little details and folds to the cloak. Glue a blue rhinestone to the front as a cloak clasp.

Then make a **hairstyle** and a large **beard** for King Winter out of white silk. To make the hair, wind the silk around the head and felt in place. Felt the beard to the lower third of the face and shape the ends.

King Winter is wearing a glittering crown and holds an icicle sceptre and an ice ball. Here's how to make his accessories.

Cut uneven points out of a 3 cm (1½ in) high strip of white cardboard. Measure the crown around the head and glue the ends together to make a ring. To make the sceptre, cut out a triangular piece of paper and wind it into a pointy cone. The ice ball is a large white bead. Apply craft glue to all the objects and sprinkle with white glitter.

This is only one way of making decorations for King Winter. You can also cut the crown out of white craft felt or metal foil. The sceptre and ball can be felted quickly out of wool. Choose the method that suits you best!

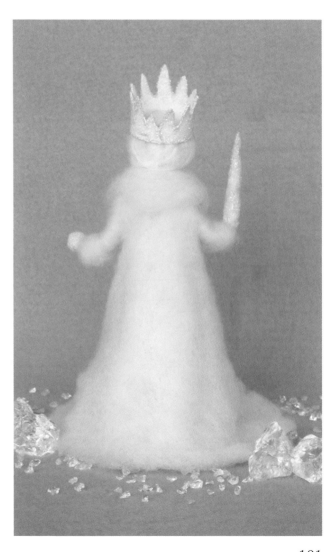

Winter princess ***

The winter princess has found a place beside King Winter in the frozen landscape – of course, you could also make a little prince. See instructions for Season's children on page 48. Make sure to add some glitter so they sparkle and stand out.

MATERIALS
- Skin-coloured wool for the body
- Pipe cleaners, one for each child, about 15 cm (6 in)
- White and light blue wool
- White wool nubs for the hair
- White beads

INSTRUCTIONS
Follow the instructions for Stable standing figures on page 30. Use the proportions for a childlike figure (see page 38). It is best to make very small children with a wool cone.

DETAILS AND DECORATIONS
Wind white wool around the arms and upper body. Wind light blue wool around the skirt cone. To make the top of the dress, take a piece of white wool about 15 cm (6 in) long and pull it over the head. Felt it lightly to the body.

Divide the skirt into equal sections and lightly felt the tips. Make curly white hair and twist it into a bun.

Decorate the dress with small beads. The winter princess is playing with a snowball – a large bead with glitter glued to it. If you want, you can make small white felt balls for snowballs.

Winter children ***

Sledging over freshly fallen snow is wonderful. The little winter children here are having great fun in the wintry landscape. The white wool makes for soft, welcoming-looking snow.

MATERIALS
- Skin-coloured wool for the body
- Pipe cleaners, about 15 cm (6 in)
- Light blue, red, yellow and white wool

INSTRUCTIONS FOR THE GIRL
Follow the instructions for Stable standing figures on page 30. Use the proportions for a childlike figure (see page 38).

DETAILS AND DECORATIONS
Wind red wool around the skirt. Wind light blue wool around the arms and upper body. Make the hands with white wool to show that the child is wearing warm gloves.

To make the coat, use a piece of light blue wool about 8 cm (3 in) long. Needle felt it in place right around the figure. Place a small amount of wool around the neck for a collar and needle felt in place.

Make a light blue hat over long blond hair for the winter child. To do this, place some blue wool over the hair and needle felt into the shape of a hat. Place some white wool around the front edge of the hat and felt in place. The blond hair is visible as a plait hanging out the back of the hat.

Tip

Instructions here are for the little girl. For the boy, see the small mermaid (page 84) but without the tail. Make him with trouser legs together, or wind around pipe cleaners to make separate legs. For more detailed instructions, see my book *Magic Wool Fruit Children*.

Mother Thaw ***

Mother Thaw represents the end of King Winter's reign. If she wins, then spring is near, and the yearly circle begins anew.

- Skin-coloured wool for the body
- One pipe cleaner, about 15 cm (6 in)
- Green and yellow-green wool for the dress
- Brown wool bat for the cape
- Dark brown wool for the hair
- Small broom (or you can bind some small twigs)
- Sewing thread and sewing needle

INSTRUCTIONS

Follow the instructions for Stable standing figures on page 30. Use the proportions for an adult figure (see page 39), with a wool or Styrofoam cone as a body core.

DETAILS AND DECORATIONS

Wind green wool completely around the arms and the upper body. Wind light brown wool around the skirt cone and felt a piece of yellow-green wool to the front as an **apron**. Wind some beige wool around the waist as the apron strings.

Make some smooth dark brown **hair**. You don't need to make a hairstyle as the mother is wearing a cape with a hood. Lay a piece of the brown wool bat around the hair and felt it on to make the hood.

To make the **cape**, take a piece of brown wool bat measuring about 17 x 13 cm (6½ x 5 in). Needle felt the bat until you have a cape shape. (Make sure your felting surface is large enough to place the entire cape over it.)

Once the cape is finished, place it over the shoulders and needle felt in place. If you like, add a decorative bead as a clasp and sew a small broom to the hand. Now Mother Thaw can sweep away the last pieces of snow.

Tip

You can find small brooms in craft stores or doll's house suppliers. Alternatively, you can make your own broom by binding up twigs with a little wool.

More Ideas

Creativity stands for:
inventing, experimenting, taking risks, breaking rules,
making mistakes and
having fun

Mary Lou Cook

Once you have completed several projects, you will be familiar with the necessary steps and it should not be too difficult to make the figures shown on the following pages. I have included these examples as a source of inspiration for your own creative ideas and to illustrate the different possibilities of the seasons' figures.

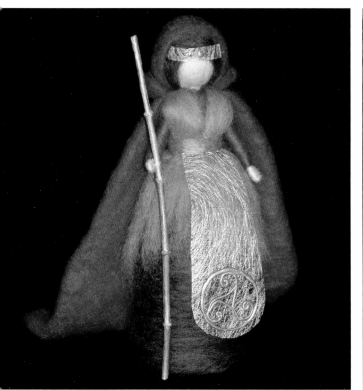

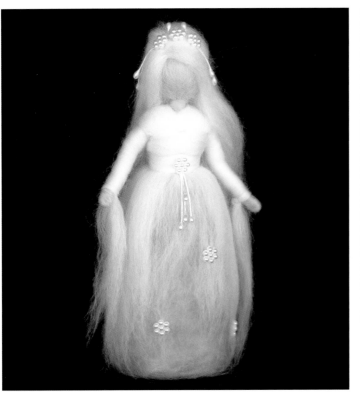

Final Word

Even a third book cannot be written alone. I would like to thank the people who supported me with advice and help:

My busy husband, for his tireless effort and the beautiful photos. He willingly photographed a second time if I was not satisfied with the first version. Thank you dear – where would I be without you?

My creative daughters, who are my harshest critics and because of this motivate me continually. Thank you for your wealth of ideas and your patience!

My computer-buff son, who is always willing to help me with the computer and over time has taught me the tips and tricks which make working with technology easier. Thank you, child – but your daily computer time is still limited!

Maria A. Kafitz, my editor from Freies Geistesleben, who makes it easy for me to write creative books and who improves them unfailingly with her perceptive vision, thank you.

Bianca Bonfert, whose creative hands assembled my loose collection of texts and pictures into a readable whole, thank you.

And finally, I would like to thank all friends and fans of my magic wool figures. Your enthusiasm and friendly letters from all over the world are a constant source of joy and motivation!

Christine Schäfer

Resources

Recommended sources for magic wool and natural materials:

AUSTRALIA
Morning Star
www.morningstarcrafts.com.au

Winterwood Toys
www.winterwoodtoys.com.au

NORTH AMERICA
The Waldorf Early Childhood Association of North America maintains an online list of suppliers at:
www.waldorfearlychildhood.org/sources.asp

UK
Myriad Natural Toys
www.myriadonline.co.uk

Further Reading

From Floris Books, Edinburgh unless otherwise stated

Adolphi, Sybille, *Making Fairy Tale Scenes*
—, *Making Flower Children*
—, *Making More Flower Children*

Almon, Joan, *First Steps in Natural Dyeing*, WECAN Publications
Berger, Petra, *Feltcraft*
Berger, Thomas, *The Christmas Craft Book*
—, *Crafts Through the Year*
—, *The Gnome Craft Book*
Dhom, Christel, *The Advent Craft and Activity Book*
Fischer, Ute, *Weaving With Children*
Grigaff, Anne-Dorthe, *Knitted Animals*, Hawthorn Press
Guéret, Frédérique, *Magical Window Stars*
Jaffke, Freya, *Celebrating Festivals with Children*
—, *Toymaking with Children.*
—, *Work and Play in Early Childhood*
Jaffke, Freya & Dagmar Schmidt, *Magic Wool*
Kutsch, Irmgard & Brigitte Walden, *Spring Nature Activities for Children* (includes activities using plant-based dyes)
—, *Winter Nature Activities for Children* (includes preparing and working with wool)
Leeuwen, M v. & J. Moeskops, *The Nature Corner: Celebrating the year's cycle with seasonal tableaux*
Neuschütz, Karin, *Creative Wool*
—, *Making Soft Toys*
—, *Sewing Dolls*
Reinhard, Rotraud, *A Felt Farm*
Schäfer, Christine, *Magic Wool Fairies*
—, *Magic Wool Fruit Children*
Wolck-Gerche, Angelika, *Creative Felt*
—, *More Magic Wool*
—, *Papercraft*

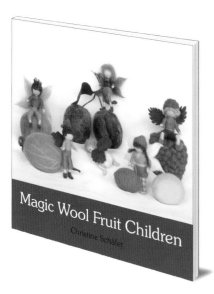

Magic Wool Fruit Children

Christine Schäfer

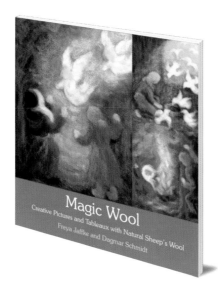

Magic Wool

Creative Pictures and Tableaux with Natural Sheep's Wool

Freya Jaffke and Dagmar Schmidt

Creative Wool

Making Woollen Crafts with Children

Karin Neuschütz

Magic Wool Fairies

Christine Schäfer

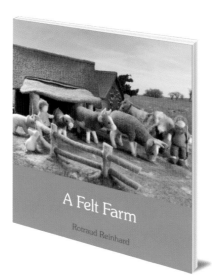

A Felt Farm

Rotraud Reinhard

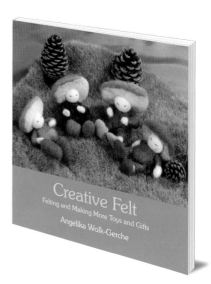

Creative Felt

Felting and Making More Toys and Gifts

Angelika Wolk-Gerche

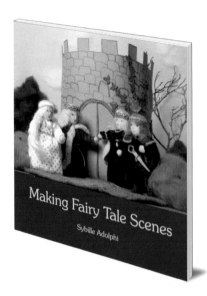

Making Fairy Tale Scenes
Sybille Adolphi

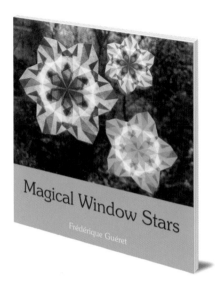

Magical Window Stars
Frédérique Guéret

Crafts Through the Year
Thomas and Petra Berger

Feltcraft
Making Dolls, Gifts and Toys
Petra Berger

Making Flower Children
Sybille Adolphi

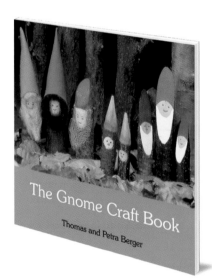

The Gnome Craft Book
Thomas and Petra Berger

Crocheting Soft Toys

Angelika Wolk-Gerche

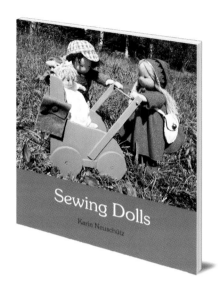

Sewing Dolls

Karin Neuschütz

Making Flower Children

Sybille Adolphi

A SWEDISH CHRISTMAS

Simple Scandinavian Crafts, Recipes and Decorations

CAROLINE WENDT AND PERNILLA WÄSTBERG

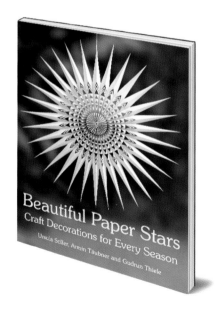

Beautiful Paper Stars

Craft Decorations for Every Season

Ursula Stiller, Armin Täubner and Gudrun Thiele

Finger Strings

A Book of Cat's-Cradles and String Figures

Michael Taylor

florisbooks.co.uk